The Best of
BANJO PATERSON

The Best of
BANJO PATERSON

Introduction by Bruce Elder

Murray Child & Company, an imprint of
MURRAY DAVID PUBLISHING

Published by
Murray Child & Company
an imprint of
MURRAY DAVID PUBLISHING PTY LTD
23 O'Connors Road, Beacon Hill, NSW, 2100, Australia
33a Carnarvon Drive, Frenchs Forest, NSW, 2086

First published 1996
Reprinted 1997

Printed by Australian Print Group, Maryborough, Victoria

ISBN 0 908048 35 1

Contents

Introduction

Andrew Barton Paterson, known affectionately as Banjo Paterson, is one of Australia's most important literary figures. His poems have transcended issues of literary greatness and creativity and become part of the folk culture of the country. They are part of the nation's mythology and imagination and, as such, are integral to the way Australians see themselves. They are authentic expressions of a people which, in its infancy, saw itself as essentially rural, hardworking, laconic, isolated and deeply individualistic. They reflect a world that no longer exists—except in the minds and the imaginations of the people.

Modern Australia is not Banjo Paterson's Australia. It is urban and suburban. Over 70 per cent of the country's population now live in the state capitals (including Canberra and Darwin), and six other major cities with populations of over 100 000, and over 85 per cent live in urban areas. Only in Queensland, Tasmania and the Northern Territory does the population in the capital represent less than 50 per cent of each region's total population.

Australia is one of the most intensely urban countries in the world. The true images of modern Australia are suburban images. The neatly mown backyard, the barbecue, the backyard swimming pool, the neat project home on a block of land that was once called 'a quarter of an acre', the television set and sound system in the lounge room, the department store furniture, the desirability of being close to a school and public transport, the need to own a car, and the weekend ritual of shopping in supermarkets are all vital aspects of the way we define ourselves as a society.

Australians also cling to the coast. There is a deep love of the beach and the ocean. In summer the beaches around the mainland state capitals are characterised by traffic jams, the smell of 15+ sunscreen oils, the sight of raw skin being parboiled until it becomes nuggetty brown and people diving into the cool, clean waters.

Beyond the coast the country is unknown. Australians talk about 'the big trip' when, usually after retiring from a lifetime of work in a city, they will buy a caravan and 'see Australia' by travelling Highway 1 and going up or down the Stuart Highway through Alice Springs and 'the inland'. For all this talk, relatively few people make the journey and even fewer really know the vast area beyond the coast. Melburnians will visit the Dandenongs and trek to the snowfields in winter; Sydneysiders venture to the Blue Mountains and know the strip of land on either side of the Hume Highway; the people of Adelaide know their hills and the state's wine-growing valleys and Brisbane residents will occasionally journey to Toowoomba.

To most Australians 'the inland' is a mythical place. It is not real, because they have not been there. It is known only through photographs, television and film, literature, painting and the stories of others. Australians have no trouble talking about the land 'beyond the black stump' because they have seen photographs of Uluru and the MacDonnell Ranges. They know the photographs of the vast emptiness of the Nullarbor and the western plains of Queensland. They also know the inland through endless television documentaries and through films as diverse as *Mad Max II* and *Walkabout*. They all know that Australia has the second largest dry desert area in the world and they know its power because, every few years, some foolish, unlucky soul runs out of petrol or gets lost and, inevitably, they die of heat exhaustion and dehydration.

In the Australian consciousness we huddle on the coast with a mysterious, mythical country behind us. We sit in our comfortable three bedroom homes, eat and laugh around backyard barbecues, absorb the popular culture of the 'global village' and pretend that we are secure. But, all the time, the great Australian loneliness, the vast inhospitable deserts with small isolated groups of Aborigines and forlorn-looking sheep and kangaroos, seems to cry out that we are strangers in a strange land.

This was not always the case. The urbanisation of Australia is a relatively modern phenomenon. At the end of the nineteenth century the outback was central to Australia's economic health. The vast sheep stations of western New South Wales and western Queensland produced wool clips which were shipped around the world. Shearers, itinerant rural workers, bullock dray drivers, Cobb & Co. coaches, stock and station agents and graziers travelled across the vast flat plains. The rivers of western New South Wales were plied by paddle steamers which made their way from South Australia up the Murray–Darling systems to inland ports like Bourke and Wagga Wagga. Bullock teams dragged heavy loads of wool from outlying sheep stations to the ports where inland Maritime Service Boards were established.

To understand this phenomenon the history of the western New South Wales town of Bourke is informative and emblematic. In 1859, Captain W. R. Randall sailed the *Gemini* up the Darling from South Australia. Overnight Bourke, Brewarrina and other centres along the river became vital transport links. For decades Bourke was the transport centre for the whole of south-west Queensland and western New South Wales. Its port was the only efficient way to transport wool to the coastal markets and at its height in the late 1880s and 1890s over 40 000 bales of wool were being shipped down the Darling annually. The river transport continued until the last commercial riverboat in 1931.

In 1862 the township was surveyed and the first businesses—Bourke Store and Bourke Hotel—were established. This was a boom time for the town with large land holdings being taken up by optimistic graziers. The unreliability of the rainfall—it averages 340 mm but is likely to vary from 150 mm one year to 800 mm the next—forced many of the optimists out of the area.

The building now known as the Government Offices was built between 1863 and 1865 as the town's first Court House. It served the town for only a decade before the second Court House was built in 1875. Today the first Court House, which has been beautifully restored, is one of the most attractive buildings in the town.

The Post Office, which was built in 1880 with the upper floor being added some years later, survived the 1890 flood (the town's worst flood when the river broke its banks and the levees which had been built) by building its own levee. Nearby is the Carriers Arms Hotel in which Henry Lawson reputedly wrote some stories and which was a popular Cobb & Co. stop-off point.

The Bourke Weir was opened in 1897 and was designed to maintain a reasonable level of water in the river near the town. The lock was nearly 60 metres long and 11 metres wide and was the only one built on the Darling.

The town was a dynamic centre from the 1860s to the 1930s. There are graves of Afghan camel drivers in the local cemetery and the grave of the bushranger Captain Moonlight is located north of the town. Today Bourke is a sleepy settlement servicing the surrounding properties and the travellers who are making their way along the highway from Sydney to western Queensland.

Somewhere in the Australian psyche places like Bourke are our 'wild west'. They are part of our romantic race memory. The idea of paddle steamers plying the Murray, of bushrangers, of Afghan camel drivers, of vast stock holdings with thousands of sheep, of men with swags on their backs walking hundreds of miles from one station to another, of hands gnarled by hard work, of shearers, ringers, jackaroos, stockmen, boundary riders and camp cooks, of billies boiling over open fires, of huge chunks of mutton for

Sunday dinner and of men breasting the bar and drinking beer and spirits is endlessly appealing. This was the world that Banjo Paterson knew, loved and wrote about. Yet it is so far removed from modern suburban life.

Two writers, more than anyone else in the history of Australian literature, have been central to the creation of this national memory—Henry Lawson and Andrew 'Banjo' Paterson. They may never have won any prestigious international literary awards. They may be considered minor poets and conventional short-story writers by international and modern standards. They may be seen as very conservative and old-fashioned, but they have had a huge impact on the way Australians see themselves.

They were born within three years of each other. Lawson, the son of a gold miner, was born at Grenfell, NSW, in 1867. Paterson, the son of a well-to-do grazier, was born three years earlier at Narrambla, near Orange, NSW. They were both products of rural Australia, yet their backgrounds couldn't have been more different. Lawson had only three years of formal schooling and was profoundly deaf by the time he was fourteen. Paterson was sent to boarding school in Sydney and, after receiving his secondary education at Sydney Grammar School, he studied law at Sydney University. Lawson came from a family of political radicals and was a passionate republican. Paterson's family were Lanarkshire farmers. Paterson's father had emigrated to Australia around 1850 and established himself in the Lachlan area where he became a prominent and well known local figure. Still, these widely different men had a passionate love of Australia and both had the talent to find a way to express their love through poetry and prose.

They both emerged as major literary figures in the late 1880s when their work was accepted for publication by the *Bulletin*. Patricia Rolfe in *The Journalistic Javelin: An Illustrated History of the Bulletin* wrote: Lawson and Paterson began writing for the *Bulletin* at much the same time...It is surprising, leafing through the *Bulletin*, to note how early they appeared and to realise how happy that appearance was...Although both went off in other directions, Lawson and Paterson were the first to give real impetus to the bush ballad in the *Bulletin*.'

In recent times critics have been dismissive of bush ballads. They have seen these vernacular 'songs' as excessively romantic, not terribly good poetry and more connected with singalong rhythms than with serious thoughts. What these critics have tended to overlook is that the bush ballad, in the hands of Paterson and Lawson, became an authentic and highly original expression of rural Australia. Stylistically they reached back to the oral and folk traditions of Europe (many felt there were connections with the Scottish border ballads) and, when combined with the folk tunes of Britain and Ireland, they gave Australians a folk music tradition which dealt with local issues and events.

It is also worth remembering that when Lawson and Paterson first started writing bush ballads for the *Bulletin* it was, as Patricia Rolfe has pointed out, 'new, unique and exciting. It was verse for the ear as well as the eye and it often carried a note of social reform'.

Rolfe explains Paterson and Lawson's involvement in detail:

> Andrew Barton Paterson's first submission to the *Bulletin*...was in 1885...His pseudonym, from what he called a 'so-called racehorse the family had had', appeared on June 12, 1886...under 'The Bush Fire, an Allegory', a mild enough satire on Gladstone and Irish Home Rule, describing a bushfire on Billy Gladstone's spread, part of which is Paddy Melon Flat. On October 30, 1886, 'A Dream of the Melbourne Cup', appeared. Next was 'The Mylora Elopement' in the Christmas issue.
>
> On March 5, 1887, Paterson published his first try at lampooning local politics, 'The Deficit Demon'. 'Old Pardon, the Son of Reprieve', was in the Christmas issue of 1888. In 1889 Paterson had poems through the year, with 'Clancy of the Overflow',' The Scapegoat' and 'The Idyll of Dandaloo' in the Christmas issue. The *Bulletin* said that Clancy was by a 'modest young man of Sydney'. Lawson had 'The Roving Days' in the same issue. When 'The Man from Snowy River' appeared in April 26, 1890, Lawson's 'The Song of Old Joe Swallow' came a month later. In the

Christmas issue that year were Paterson's 'On Kiley's Run' and 'The Story of Conroy's Gap'.

Through the late 1880s Lawson and Paterson became the *Bulletin*'s two pre-eminent poets. They seemed to be in competition and, as this perceived competition grew, Sydney's small literary community began taking sides. In a typically Australian act of egalitarianism most people sided with poor Lawson against the wealthier and better educated Paterson. But, like most literary arguments, the basis of the anti-Paterson prejudice was unjustified. Paterson may have been wealthy but he also knew and loved the bush. He was an excellent rider, he knew the folk legends of the bush, and he had a keen eye for the details of bush life. This anti-Paterson was probably an early example of the 'tall poppy' syndrome because, while Lawson enjoyed moderate commercial success, Paterson was 'a hit'. His book of ballads *The Man from Snowy River and Other Verses* was published in 1895 and, within a year, had sold over 10 000 copies. George Robertson, of Angus & Robertson, wrote to Paterson concerning the publication of the *The Man from Snowy River* 'You will be glad to hear that Snowy River has beaten the record in Australian publishing...we intend going on with a second edition at once. We expected that we would require to go to press again this year, but did not calculate on having to do it before the publication of the first edition. It will not be published until Saturday—such a thing has never happened in Australia we think.' He was the Morris West or Colleen McCullough of his age and, as such, inevitably attracted detractors.

But the Banjo's bush credentials were impeccable. Patricia Rolfe tells the story of a man from Wee Jasper who said of Paterson: 'Banjo was a great bushman. I never saw a man who could rough it better. Out camping, mustering on the mountains, he would lie on a ground sheet with a blanket over him, or a sheet of bark covered by a blanket. Once over, and he would snore all night.'

Throughout Paterson's life there were people claiming that they were the model for the characters in his poems. There were literally dozens of claimants to the title 'Man from Snowy River'. The ballad writer Charles Souter said that he had met an old bushie in the 1880s who had claimed that any letter addressed to 'Clancy of the Overflow' would get to him, and for years controversy has raged over who the real role model for the swagman in 'Waltzing Matilda' was.

In the latter case, which is undoubtedly Paterson's most famous poem, the argument is an attempt to turn myth into reality. No one knows exactly what prompted Paterson to write his tale of the swaggie who, rather than surrender to the police, decided to commit suicide by jumping into a billabong. However the blurry pieces of the puzzle are intriguing.

On 4 September 1894 the *Brisbane Courier* reported: 'Information has been received at Winton that a man named Hoffmeister, a prominent unionist, was found dead about two miles from Kynuna. The local impression is that he was one of the attacking mob at Dagworth and was wounded there. There were seven unionists with Hoffmeister when he died. These assert that he committed suicide.'

It is now widely believed that this story was the inspiration for the song, although the Winton town history (published in 1975) offers a more romantic version.

Paterson was staying at Dagworth Station (the ruins are located approximately 100 kilometres north-west of Winton) in 1895 when Christina Macpherson played the tune 'Craiglea' for the guests. Paterson liked the tune and inquired about the words. Macpherson explained that she did not know of any words. This was enough to inspire Paterson.

The lyrics which he wrote were an intermingling of a series of events which occurred while he was staying at Dagworth Station. During his stay Paterson saw a sheep which appeared to have died but on closer examination it had been killed, presumably by a swagman, and portions of it carefully removed to give the impression of natural death. This was possibly the inspiration for 'the crime'.

A second strand to the story focuses on Combo Waterhole. This waterhole on Belfast Station, 145 kilometres north-west of Winton, is clearly the setting for the poem. It is argued that Paterson used the setting after he had been told the story of Hoffmeister at

Combo Waterhole by Robert Macpherson. There has been some suggestion that the story Paterson heard was not about Hoffmeister but about an unknown swagman and a stockman named Harry Wood. Wood had beaten an Aboriginal boy named Charlie to death and the Winton police, while trying to locate him, happened upon the swagman sitting by the billabong.

It is also claimed that the expression 'Waltzing Matilda' was first mentioned to Paterson at Dagworth Station by a jackeroo named Jack Carter.

In a letter to the *Australian* in 1995, at the time of the centenary celebrations of 'Waltzing Matilda', Dr Ross Fitzgerald, Associate Professor of History and Politics at Griffith University in Queensland, stated quite categorically:

> The song was written by Banjo Paterson in January 1895 just fourteen weeks after an armed battle at Dagworth woolshed in September 1894 between striking shearers and the station owners, the Macphersons. In the 'Battle of Dagworth' 140 lambs were burnt to death, while one of the sixteen striking insurrectionists, Samuel 'French' Hoffmeister died, supposedly by committing suicide, beside a billabong near Macpherson's Dagworth Station.
>
> Banjo visited the homestead shortly after the battle. While the site of old Dagworth Station where Banjo stayed is now a heap of rubble, thanks to Richard Magoffin's brilliant detective work Samuel Hoffmeister's grave at Kynuna Station, on the southern side of the Diamantina River, has been discovered, and a stone cairn placed beside the billabong. The three policemen involved have been revealed to be Senior Constables Austin Cafferty (number 420), Michael Daly, (89), and Robert Dyer (175).
>
> It is clear that Miss Christina Macpherson, who had heard the Scottish tune Craigilee played by a band at the annual Steeplechase race meeting at Warrnambool, Victoria, in April 1884, met Paterson when he visited her brother, Bob Macpherson, at Dagworth. There being no piano at the homestead, the tune that Christina had memorised she played to him on an autoharp, which is like a zither. To this tune, as Magoffin and Clement Semmler demonstrate, Banjo added the words to the song 'Waltzing Matilda', just fourteen weeks after the Battle at Dagworth Station.
>
> It is important to note that in the original verses the swagman was camped in, not by, the billabong and that there were three policemen, not—as one theory has it—one fictitious trooper 'number 123'....Contrary to the sanitised version of the so-called 'jolly swagman', which did not exist in Paterson's original version, 'Waltzing Matilda' is actually a powerful political allegory based on the 1894 Shearers' Strike.

Whatever the real origins of the events and the images, Paterson wrote the song and it received its first public performance at the North Gregory Hotel in Winton. The current hotel is the fourth North Gregory (the other three either burned down or were destroyed) but it is still on the location of the original pub. From photographs the original North Gregory was a modest building with little more than bark walls and a corrugated iron roof.

The swagman has been immortalised, albeit in fibreglass, beside the swimming pool in Winton. Appropriately, he sits near a very healthy looking coolabah tree.

But Banjo Paterson's work is much more than 'Waltzing Matilda'. It should, however, be recognised that 'Waltzing Matilda', like so many of Paterson's poems, has become part of Australian folklore. We know and treasure these images and see them as part of our cultural heritage.

Until relatively recently Banjo Paterson was an integral part of every Australian school student's education. He was not someone who was formally taught in senior High School English Literature courses. He was a poet whose works were read aloud to generations of primary school children by teachers who seemed to know the words by heart. His famous poems were illustrated and the works were readily available in school libraries and in school magazines. The simplicity of his rhyme schemes were such that his poems were easy to remember.

But how good was Paterson as a poet? The fair

answer is that while he was clearly a romantic and a sentimentalist he was a writer with a finely developed sense of a memorable image, a wonderful sense of the rhythms of the bush, and the rare ability to write about people who, over the intervening years, have become Australian archetype—the loner, the little battler, the rustic innocent. Each of these qualities have made him special. It doesn't matter whether he's writing in a humorous vein or trying to evoke a world he loved—at his best he is quintessentially Australian. His poems have little meaning to people beyond Australia's shores.

Anyone who has spent an extended time in the Snowy Mountains (I grew up there and feel that I can speak with some authority) knows that when he writes:

And down by Kosciusko, where the pine-clad ridges raise
Their torn and rugged battlements on high,
Where the air is clear as crystal, and the white stars fairly blaze
At midnight in the cold and frosty sky,

he is, with great precision and with a painter's eye for detail, conjuring up the beauty of the Snowy Mountains. This may not be poetry heavy with imagery but it is evocative of the place.

Similarly the rhythms of 'The Man from Snowy River', particularly within the constraints of the bush ballad form, are superb. There is a wonderful forward momentum. A sense of the speed and the smell of the horses is captured. There is a sense of the beauty of the movement of the animals. It is quite impossible to read the lines:

He sent the flint stones flying, but the pony kept his feet,
He cleared the fallen timber in his stride,
And the man from Snowy River never shifted in his seat—
It was grand to see that mountain horseman ride.
Through the stringybarks and saplings, on the rough and broken ground,
Down the hillside at a racing pace he went;
And he never drew the bridle till he landed safe and sound,
At the bottom of that terrible descent.

without becoming physically involved in this hair-raising piece of daredevil riding. This is great descriptive poetry. Everything is in place. The rhythm is right, the descriptions are evocative, the excitement of the chase is captured.

Beyond this the central theme of 'The Man from Snowy River'—the victory of the poor battler over the acknowledged masters and the courage of the little man—is deeply rooted in the Australian psyche. It is a national quality we are proud of. As a nation we love to see the 'tall poppies', the rich and the successful, get their comeuppance and we love nothing more than to see this done by somebody who has never enjoyed the advantages of wealth and privilege. It is part of our egalitarian heritage. What Paterson does in the poem is create a genuine Australian myth. The contrasts are simply and clearly drawn. On one side there are 'the tried and noted riders from the stations near and far' including Harrison—'few could ride beside him when his blood was fairly up'—and Clancy—'no better horseman ever held the reins'. On the other side is the classic underdog—'And one was there, a stripling on a small and weedy beast'—who is even dismissed by Harrison who says 'That horse will never do / For a long and tiring gallop—lad you'd better stop away, Those hills are far too rough for such as you.'

In a very real sense the ending is inevitable. Of course the 'stripling' will win. That is the stuff of myths. Still, Paterson manages to weave a spell around the reader and we are taken on a journey which is both cinematic in its visual power and moving in its sense of triumph and pride. We participate in the experience.

In many ways the 'The Geebung Polo Club' deals with similar issues. The theme of the triumph of the underdog is expanded to include the eternal conflict and rivalry between town and country. Again this is pure myth. These themes are common in both the Bible and *Aesop's Fables.* The triumph of the underdog is really nothing more than a modern reworking of the story of David and Goliath. The Geebung Polo

Club is the timeless story of the town mouse and the country mouse.

It was somewhere up the country, in a land of rock and scrub,
That was formed an institution called the Geebung Polo Club.
They were long and wiry natives from the rugged mountainside,
And the horse was never saddled that the Geebungs couldn't ride;
But their style of playing polo was irregular and rash—
They had mighty little science, but a mighty lot of dash:
And they played on mountain ponies that were muscular and strong,
Though their coats were quite unpolished, and their manes and tails were long
And they used to train their ponies wheeling cattle in the scrub:
They were demons, were the members of the Geebung Polo Club.

Paterson's imagery drives home the central message of the poem. The land is rough 'rock and scrub', the locals are 'wiry', their style is 'irregular and rash', their horses are 'quite unpolished'. The effect is to create a world of raw rural roughness. There is no doubt where Paterson's sympathies lie. This is a world he admires and loves. We know that the city slickers from the 'Cuff and Collar Team' with be the exact opposite—and, of course, they are. Their members are 'exclusive' and they have 'natty little ponies that were nice, and smooth, and sleek'. His language indicates that he sees them as a bunch of toffs who deserve to be taken apart by the men from the bush. The fact that the game ends in a draw is a comment on Paterson's belief that people from the bush aren't better, they're simply different.

This city–country conflict reached a wonderful high point in the hilarious, and much loved, 'Man from Ironbark'. Again Paterson appears to take sides. His description of the barber and the city slickers in the barber's shop is unambiguous and suitably satiric.

The barber was small and flash, as barbers mostly are,
He wore a strike-your-fancy sash, he smoked a huge cigar;
and
There were some gilded youths that sat along the barber's wall.
Their eyes were dull, their heads were flat, they had no brains at all;

Poems like this work because, apart from being very funny, they are more like jokes or anecdotes. They tell simple stories with simple messages but the messages are seen by the reader to be true reflections of something deeper and more complex. The bush man, the man from Ironbark, is a simpleton with simple solutions. He's rough and crude but he is also a man of integrity and honesty. The city barber, and his 'gilded youths' are seen as representing a sophisticated but shallow world full of dubious moral and social values.

In the late nineteenth century, when the coastal cities were growing rapidly and there was talk of the states uniting to become the new country of Australia, these contrasts were often discussed. There was a feeling that Australia, for most of the nineteenth century, had relied upon the bush and now it was starting to change. This was partly true. The wealth of the country had been a combination of sheep, wheat and gold. The growth of the great coastal cities had been a direct result of the success of the farmers and the miners. The wealth of Melbourne had been created almost entirely by the wealth of the Victorian goldfields and the wealth of Sydney was a reflection of the success of graziers in New South Wales. The people in the country may have been simple and crude but they were honest, hard-working and vital to the country's economic health. The people in the city may seem sophisticated. They may look down their noses at the country bumpkins. But they had no right.

Paterson captured this conflict with just the right level of humour and ambiguity to ensure that he offended neither side. In the process he managed subtly to recognise the virtues of the bush. There is perhaps no better example of this than 'A Bush Christening' which first appeared in the *Bulletin* on

16 December 1893. The poem opens:

On the outer Barcoo where the churches are few,
And men of religion are scanty,
On a road never cross'd 'cept by folk that are lost,
One Michael Magee had a shanty.

Listen to the rhythms and you can hear the slowness of bush life, the flattened vowels and the nasally twang of outback Australia. It is impossible to read 'On the outer Barcoo where the churches are few' without a wry, bucolic smile just as it is impossible to read 'He sent the flint stones flying, but the pony kept his feet,' without feeling the energy and excitement.

Equally, although the poem is humorous and light hearted, there is something plaintive about 'On a road never cross'd 'cept by folk that are lost'. It is a simple, but powerful, description of the loneliness and isolation of the outback. Of course, the 'ten-year-old lad' who is about to be christened is out of the man from Ironbark school of bucolic fools. He is not used to city ways. He has never seen a preacher and he certainly doesn't understand what a christening is. Still this is a world to be admired—for all its foolishness and innocence.

So, what kind of man wrote these poems. Banjo Paterson was one of those lucky people who instinctively hear the voice of the people. He had been a lawyer but, with the success of his poetry in the *Bulletin*, he abandoned law and for most of the rest of his life moved between journalism and poetry. He worked for the *Sydney Morning Herald* as a war correspondent during the Boer War and travelled to China. In the first decade of this century he was the editor of both the *Sydney Evening News* (1904-06) and the *Town and Country Journal* (1907-08). During this period he edited a collection of Australian songs, *The Old Bush Songs* (1905) and wrote a novel, *An Outback Marriage* (1906). In short, from the 1880s until 1908, he was a professional writer whose work ranged from anthologies to poetry, journalism, essay writing, war correspondent, novelist and editor. In spite of this rich diversity of writing skills he never escaped from his reputation as a writer of bush ballads.

In 1908 he sold the rights to his poems and with the money bought a property near Yass on the upper Murrumbidgee in New South Wales. He was not a successful grazier; however, he remained on the land until 1914 when, with the outbreak of war, he sailed to Europe hoping, once again, to become a war correspondent. After the war he settled in Sydney and continued to work as a journalist. It is significant that, although he continued to be both prolific and successful, all the works for which he is best remembered were written in the short period between the late 1880s and the turn of the century.

Paterson died in Sydney on 5 February 1941. In retrospect he had enjoyed a full and interesting life. He had been a successful and prosperous writer. His major work had been rooted in his love of the Australian bush. He had been able to write about the people, the sounds, the smells and the scenery in a way that allowed ordinary Australians an opportunity to look into the heartland of their continent. He was a myth maker who helped to define the nature of modern Australia.

BRUCE ELDER

The Best of

BANJO PATERSON

A Dream of the Melbourne Cup (1886)

Bring me a quart of colonial beer
And some doughy damper to make good cheer,
   I must make a heavy dinner;
Heavily dine and heavily sup,
Of indigestible things fill up,
Next month they run the Melbourne Cup,
   And I have to dream the winner.

Stoke it in, boys! the half-cooked ham,
The rich ragout and the charming cham.,
   I've got to mix my liquor;
Give me a gander's gaunt hind leg,
Hard and tough as a wooden peg,
And I'll keep it down with a hard-boiled egg,
   'Twill make me dream the quicker.

Now that I'm full of fearful feed,
Oh, but I'll dream of a winner indeed
   In my restless, troubled slumber;
While the night-mares race through my heated brain
And their devil-riders spur amain,
The tip for the Cup will reward my pain,
   And I'll spot the winning number.

Thousands and thousands and thousands more,
Like sands on the white Pacific shore,
The crowding people cluster;
For evermore, it's the story old
While races are bought and backers are sold,
Drawn by the greed of the gain of gold,
In their thousands still they muster.

And the bookies' cries grow fierce and hot,
'I'll lay the Cup! The double, if not!'
'Five monkeys, Little John, sir!'
'Here's fives bar one, I lay, I lay!'
And so they shout through the livelong day,
And stick to the game that is sure to pay,
While fools put money on, sir!

And now in my dream I seem to go
And bet with a 'book' that I seem to know—
A Hebrew money-lender;
A million to five is the price I get—
Not bad! but before I book the bet
The horse's name I clean forget,
Its number and even gender.

Now for the start, and here they come,
And the hoof-strokes roar like a mighty drum
Beat by a hand unsteady;
They come like a rushing, roaring flood,
Hurrah for the speed of the Chester blood;
For Acme is making the pace so good
There are some of 'em done already.

But round the back she begins to tire,
And a mighty shout goes up 'Crossfire!'
The magpie jacket's leading;
And Crossfire challenges, fierce and bold,
And the lead she'll have and the lead she'll hold,
But at length gives way to the black and gold,
Which right to the front is speeding.

Carry them on and keep it up—
A flying race is the Melbourne Cup,
You must race, and stay, to win it;
And old Commotion, Victoria's pride,
Now takes the lead with his raking stride,
And a mighty roar goes far and wide—
'There's only Commotion in it!'

But one draws out from the beaten ruck
And up on the rails by a piece of luck
He comes in a style that's clever;
'It's Trident! Trident! Hurrah for Hales!'
'Go at 'em now while their courage fails;'
Trident! Trident! for New South Wales!'
The blue and white for ever!'

Under the whip! with the ears flat back,
Under the whip! though the sinews crack
No sign of the base white feather;
Stick to it now for your breeding's sake,
Stick to it now though your hearts should break,
While the yells and roars make the grand-stand shake,
They come down the straight together.

Trident slowly forges ahead,
The fierce whips cut and the spurs are red,
The pace is undiminished;
Now for the Panics that never fail!
But many a backer's face grows pale
As old Commotion swings his tail
And swerves—and the Cup is finished.

* * *

And now in my dream it all comes back:
I bet my coin on the Sydney crack,
A million I've won, no question!
'Give me my money, you hook-nosed hog!
Give me my money, bookmaking dog!'
But he disappeared in a kind of fog,
And I woke with 'the indigestion'.

The Mylora Elopement

By the winding Wollondilly where the weeping willows weep,
And the shepherd, with his billy, half awake and half asleep,
Folds his fleecy flocks that linger homewards in the setting sun,
Lived my hero, Jim the Ringer, 'cocky' on Mylora Run.

Jimmy loved the super's daughter, Miss Amelia Jane McGrath,
Long and earnestly he sought her, but he feared her stern papa;
And Amelia loved him truly—but the course of love, if true,
Never yet ran smooth or duly, as I think it ought to do.

Pondering o'er his predilection, Jimmy watched McGrath, the boss,
Riding past his lone selection, looking for a station 'oss
That was running in the ranges with a mob of outlaws wild.
Mac the time of day exchanges—off goes Jim to see his child;

Says, 'The old man's after Stager, which he'll find is no light job,
And to-morrow I will wager he will try and yard the mob.
Will you come with me to-morrow? I will let the parson know,
And for ever, joy or sorrow, he will join us here below.

'I will bring my nags so speedy, Crazy Jane and Tambourine,
One more kiss—don't think I'm greedy—good-bye, lass, before I'm seen—
Just one more—God bless you, dearie! Don't forget to meet me here,
Life without you is but weary; now, once more, good-bye, my dear.'

* * *

The daylight shines on figures twain
That ride across Mylora plain,
Laughing and talking—Jim and Jane.
'Steadily, darling. There's lots of time,
Didn't we slip the old man prime!
I knew he'd tackle that Bowneck mob,
I reckon he'll find it too big a job.
'They've beaten us all. I had a try,
But the warrigal devils seem to fly.
That Sambo's a real good bit of stuff
No doubt, but not quite good enough.
He'll have to gallop the livelong day,
To cut and come, to race and stay.

I hope he yards 'em, 'twill do him good;
To see us going I don't think would.'
A turn in the road and, fair and square,
They meet the old man standing there.
'What's up?' 'Why, running away, of course,'
Says Jim, emboldened. The old man turned,
His eye with wild excitement burned.
'I've raced all day through the scorching heat
After old Bowneck; and now I'm beat.
But over that range I think you'll find
The Bowneck mob all run stone-blind.
Will you go, and leave the mob behind?
Which will you do? Take the girl away,
Or ride like a white man should to-day,
And yard old Bowneck? Go or stay?'
Says Jim, 'I can't throw this away,
We can bolt some other day, of course—
Amelia Jane, get off that horse!
Up you get, Old Man. Whoop, halloo!
Here goes to put old Bowneck through!'
Two distant specks on the mountain-side,
Two stockwhips echoing far and wide …
Amelia Jane sat down and cried.

* * *

'Sakes, Amelia, what's up now?
Leading old Sambo, too, I vow,
And him deadbeat. Where have you been?
"Bolted with Jim!" What *do* you mean?
' "Met the old man with Sambo, licked
From running old Bowneck." Well I'm kicked—
"Ran 'em till Sambo nearly dropped?"
What did Jim do when you were stopped?
Did you bolt from father across the plain?
"Jim made you get off Crazy Jane!
And father got on and away again
The two of 'em went to the ranges grim."
Good boy, Jimmy! Oh, well done, Jim!
They're sure to get them now, of course,
That Tambourine is a spanking horse.
And Crazy Jane is good as gold.
And Jim, they say, rides pretty bold—
Not like your father, but very fair.
Jim will have to follow the mare.'
'It never was yet in father's hide
To best my Jim on the mountain-side.
Jim can rally, and Jim can ride.'
But here again Amelia cried.

* * *

The sound of a whip comes faint and far,
A rattle of hoofs, and here they are,
In all their tameless pride.
The fleet wild horses snort with fear,
And wheel and break as the yard draws near.
Now, Jim the Ringer, ride!
Wheel 'em! wheel 'em! Whoa back there, whoa!
And the foam-flakes fly like the driven snow,
As under the whip the horses go
Adown the mountain side.
And Jim, hands down, and teeth firm set,
On a horse that never has failed him yet,
Is after them down the range.
Well ridden! well ridden! they wheel—whoa back!
And long and loud the stockwhips crack,

Their flying course they change;
'Steadily does it—let Sambo go!
Open those sliprails down below.
Smart! or you'll be too late.
They'll follow old Sambo up—look out!
Wheel that black horse—give Sam a clout.
They're in! Make fast the gate.'

*　*　*

The mob is safely in the yard!
The old man mounts delighted guard.
No thought has he but for his prize ...
Jim catches poor Amelia's eyes.
'Will you come after all? The job is done,
And Crazy Jane is fit to run
For a prince's life—now don't say no;
Slip on while the old man's down below
At the inner yard, and away we'll go.
Will you come, my girl?' 'I will, you bet;
We'll manage this here elopement yet.'

*　*　*

By the winding Wollondilly stands the hut of Ringer Jim.
And his loving little Meely makes a perfect god of him.
He has stalwart sons and daughters, and, I think, before he's done,
There'll be numerous 'Six-fortys' taken on Mylora run.

Only a Jockey

'Richard Bennison, a jockey, aged 14, while riding William Tell in his training,' was thrown and killed. Luckily the horse is uninjured.'—Melbourne Wire.

Out in the grey cheerless chill of the morning light,
Out on the track where the night shades still lurk;
Ere the first gleam of the sungod's returning light,
Round come the racehorses early at work.

Reefing and pulling and racing so readily,
Close sit the jockey-boys holding them hard,
'Steady the stallion there—canter him steadily,
Don't let him gallop so much as a yard.'

Fiercely he fights while the others run wide of him,
Reefs at the bit that would hold him in thrall,
Plunges and bucks till the boy that's astride of him
Goes to the ground with a terrible fall.

'Stop him there! Block him there! Drive him in carefully,
Lead him about till he's quiet and cool.
Sound as a bell! though he's blown himself fearfully,
Now let us pick up this poor little fool.

'Stunned? Oh, by Jove, I'm afraid it's a case with him;
Ride for the doctor! keep bathing his head!
Send for a cart to go down to our place with him'—
No use! One long sigh and the little chap's dead.

Only a jockey-boy, foul-mouthed and bad you see,
Ignorant, heathenish, gone to his rest.
Parson or Presbyter, Pharisee, Sadducee,
What did you do for him?—bad was the best.

Negroes and foreigners, all have a claim on you;
Yearly you send your well-advertised hoard,
But the poor jockey-boy—shame on you, shame on you,
'Feed ye, my little ones'—what said the Lord?

Him ye held less than the outer barbarian,
Left him to die in his ignorant sin;
Have you no principles, humanitarian?
Have you no precept—'go gather them in?'

Knew he God's name? In his brutal profanity,
That name was an oath—out of many but one—
What did he get from our famed Christianity?
Where has his soul—if he had any—gone?

Fourteen years of old, and what was he taught of it?
What did he know of God's infinite grace?
Draw the dark curtain of shame o'er the thought of it,
Draw the shroud over the jockey-boy's face.

Over the Range

Little bush maiden, wondering-eyed,
Playing alone in the creek-bed dry,
In the small green flat on every side
Walled in by the Moonbi ranges high;
Tell us the tale of your lonely life,
'Mid the great grey forests that know no change.
'I never have left my home,' she said,
'I have never been over the Moonbi Range.

'Father and mother are both long dead,
And I live with granny in yon wee place.'
'Where are your father and mother?' we said.
She puzzled awhile with thoughtful face,
Then a light came into the shy brown eye,
And she smiled, for she thought the question strange
On a thing so certain—'When people die
They go to the country over the range.'

'And what is this country like, my lass?'
'There are blossoming trees and pretty flowers,
And shining creeks where the golden grass
Is fresh and sweet from the summer showers.
They never need work, nor want, nor weep;
No troubles can come their hearts to estrange.
Some summer night I shall fall asleep,
And wake in the country over the range.'

Child, you are wise in your simple trust,
For the wisest man knows no more than you
Ashes to ashes, and dust to dust:
Our views by a range are bounded too;
But we know that God hath this gift in store,
That when we come to the final change,
We shall meet with our loved ones gone before
To the beautiful country over the range.

Lost

'He ought to be home,' said the old man, 'without there's something amiss.
He only went to the Two-mile—he ought to be back by this.
He *would* ride the Reckless filly, he *would* have his wilful way;
And, here, he's not back as sundown—and what will his mother say?

'He was always his mother's idol, since ever his father died;
And there isn't a horse on the station that he isn't game to ride.
But that Reckless mare is vicious, and if once she gets away
He hasn't got the strength to hold her—and what will his mother say?'

The old man walked to the sliprail, and peered up the dark'ning track,
And looked and longed for the rider that would never more come back;
And the mother came and clutched him, with sudden, spasmodic fright:
'What has become of my Willie—why isn't he home to-night?'

Away in the gloomy ranges, at the foot of an ironbark,
The bonnie, winsome laddie was lying stiff and stark;

For the Reckless mare had smashed him against a leaning limb,
And his comely face was battered, and his merry eyes were dim.

And the thoroughbred chestnut filly, the saddle beneath her flanks,
Was away like fire through the ranges to join the wild mob's ranks;
And a broken-hearted woman and an old man worn and grey
Were searching all night in the ranges till the sunrise brought the day.

And the mother kept feebly calling, with a hope that would not die,
'Willie! where are you, Willie?' But how can the dead reply;
And hope died out with the daylight, and the darkness brought despair,
God pity the stricken mother, and answer the widow's prayer!

Though far and wide they sought him, they found not where he fell;
For the ranges held him precious, and guarded their treasure well.
The wattle blooms above him, and the blue bells blow close by,
And the brown bees buzz the secret, and the wild birds sing reply.

But the mother pined and faded, and cried, and took no rest,
And rode each day to the ranges on her hopeless weary quest.
Seeking her loved one ever, she faded and pined away,
But with strength of her great affection she still sought every day.

'I know that sooner or later I shall find my boy,' she said.
But she came not home one evening, and they found her lying dead,
And stamped on the poor pale features, as the spirit homeward pass'd,
Was an angel smile of gladness—she had found the boy at last.

Our Mat

It came from the prison this morning,
Close-twisted, neat-lettered, and flat;
It lies the hall doorway adorning,
A very good style of a mat.

Prison-made! how the spirit is moven
As we think of its story of dread—
What wiles of the wicked are woven
And spun in its intricate thread!

The letters are new, neat and nobby,
Suggesting a masterly hand—
Was it Sikes, who half-murdered the bobby,
That put the neat D on the 'and'?

Some banker found guilty of *laches*—
It's always called *laches, you* know—
Had Holt any hand in those Hs?
Did Bertrand illumine that O?

That T has a look of the gallows,
That A's a triangle, I guess;
Was it one of the Mount Rennie fellows
Who twisted the strands of the S?

Was it made by some 'highly connected',
Who is doing his spell 'on his head',
Or some wretched woman detected
In stealing her children some bread?

Does it speak of a bitter repentance
For the crime that so easily came?
Of the wearisome length of the sentence,
Of the sin, and the sorrow, and shame?

A mat! I should call it a sermon
On sin, to all sinners addressed;
It would take a keen judge to determine
Whether writer or reader is best.

Though the doorway be hard as a pavestone,
I rather would use it than that—
I'd as soon wipe my boots on a gravestone,
As I would on that Darlinghurst mat!

Old Pardon, the Son of Reprieve

You never heard tell of the story?
Well, now, I can hardly believe!
Never heard of the honour and glory
Of Pardon, the son of Reprieve?
But maybe you're only a Johnnie
And don't know a horse from a hoe?
Well, well, don't get angry, my sonny,
But, really, a young 'un should know.

They bred him out back on the 'Never',
His mother was Mameluke breed.
To the front—and then stay there—was ever
The root of the Mameluke creed.
He seemed to inherit their wiry
Strong frames—and their pluck to receive—
As hard as a flint and as fiery
Was Pardon, the son of Reprieve.

We ran him at many a meeting
At crossing and gully and town,
And nothing could give him a beating—
At least when our money was down.
For weight wouldn't stop him, nor distance,
Nor odds, though the others were fast,
He'd race with a dogged persistence,
And wear them all down at the last.

At the Turon the Yattendon filly
Led by lengths at the mile-and-a-half,
And we all began to look silly,
While *her* crowd were starting to laugh;
But the old horse came faster and faster,
His pluck told its tale, and his strength,
He gained on her, caught her, and passed her,
And won it, hands-down, by a length.

And then we swooped down on Menindie
To run for the President's Cup
Oh! that's a sweet township—a shindy
To them is board, lodging, and sup.
Eye-openers they are, and their system
Is never to suffer defeat;
It's 'win, tie, or wrangle'—to best 'em
You must lose 'em, or else it's 'dead heat'.

We strolled down the township and found 'em
At drinking and gaming and play;
If sorrows they had, why they drowned 'em,
And betting was soon under way.
Their horses were good 'uns and fit 'uns,
There was plenty of cash in the town;
They backed their own horses like Britons,
And, Lord! how *we* rattled it down!

With gladness we thought of the morrow,
We counted our wagers with glee,
A simile homely to borrow—
'There was plenty of milk in our tea.'

You see we were green; and we never
 Had even a thought of foul play,
Though we well might have known that the clever
 Division would 'put us away.'

Experience *docet,* they tell us,
 At least so I've frequently heard,
But, 'dosing' or 'stuffing,' those fellows
 Were up to each move on the board;
They got to his stall—it is sinful
 To think what such villains would do—
And they gave him a regular skinful
 Of barley—green barley—to chew.

He munched it all night, and we found him
 Next morning as full as a hog—
The girths wouldn't nearly meet round him;
 He looked like an overfed frog.
We saw we were done like a dinner—
 The odds were a thousand to one
Against Pardon turning up winner,
 'Twas cruel to ask him to run.

We got to the course with our troubles,
 A crestfallen couple were we;
And we heard the 'books' calling the doubles—
 A roar like the surf of the sea;
And over the tumult and louder
 Rang 'Any price Pardon, I lay!'
Says Jimmy, 'The children of Judah
 Are out on the warpath to-day.'

Three miles in three heats:—Ah, my sonny,
 The horses in those days were stout,
They had to run well to win money;
 I don't see such horses about.
Your six-furlong vermin that scamper
 Half-a-mile with their feather-weight up;
They wouldn't earn much of their damper
 In a race like the President's Cup.

The first heat was soon set a-going;
 The Dancer went off to the front;
The Don on his quarters was showing,
 With Pardon right out of the hunt.
He rolled and he weltered and wallowed—
 You'd kick your hat faster, I'll bet;
They finished all bunched, and he followed
 All lathered and dripping with sweat.

But troubles came thicker upon us,
 For while we were rubbing him dry
The stewards came over to warn us:
 'We hear you are running a bye!
If Pardon don't spiel like tarnation
 And win the next heat—if he can—
He'll earn a disqualification;
 Just think over *that,* now, my man!'

Our money all gone and our credit,
 Our horse couldn't gallop a yard;
And then people thought that we did it!
 It really was terribly hard.
We were objects of mirth and derision
 To folk in the lawn and the stand,
And the yells of the clever division
 Of 'Any price Pardon!' were grand.

We still had a chance for the money,
 Two heats still remained to be run;
If both fell to us—why, my sonny,
 The clever division were done.
And Pardon was better, we reckoned,
 His sickness was passing away,
So he went to the post for the second
 And principal heat of the day.

They're off and away with a rattle,
 Like dogs from the leashes let slip,
And right at the back of the battle
 He followed them under the whip.
They gained ten good lengths on him quickly
 He dropped right away from the pack;
I tell you it made me feel sickly
 To see the blue jacket fall back.

Our very last hope had departed—
 We thought the old fellow was done,
When all of a sudden he started
 To go like a shot from a gun.

His chances seemed slight to embolden
Our hearts; but, with teeth firmly set,
We thought, 'Now or never! The old 'un
May reckon with some of 'em yet.'

Then loud rose the war-cry for Pardon;
He swept like the wind down the dip,
And over the rise by the garden,
The jockey was done with the whip
The field were at sixes and sevens—
The pace at the first had been fast—
And hope seemed to drop from the heavens,
For Pardon was coming at last.

And how he did come! It was splendid;
He gained on them yards every bound,
Stretching out like a greyhound extended,
His girth laid right down on the ground.
A shimmer of silk in the cedars
As into the running they wheeled,
And out flashed the whips on the leaders,
For Pardon had collared the field.

Then right through the ruck he came sailing—
I knew that the battle was won—
The son of Haphazard was failing,
The Yattendon filly was done;
He cut down the Don and the Dancer,
He raced clean away from the mare—
He's in front! Catch him now if you can, sir!
And up went my hat in the air!

Then loud from the lawn and the garden
Rose offers of 'Ten to one *on!*'
'Who'll bet on the field? I back Pardon!'
No use; all the money was gone.
He came for the third heat light-hearted,
A-jumping and dancing about;

The others were done ere they started
Crestfallen, and tired, and worn out.

He won it, and ran it much faster
Than even the first, I believe
Oh, he was the daddy, the master,
Was Pardon, the son of Reprieve.
He showed 'em the method to travel—
The boy sat as still as a stone—
They never could see him for gravel;
He came in hard-held, and alone.

But he's old—and his eyes are grown hollow;
Like me, with my thatch of the snow;
When he dies, then I hope I may follow,
And go where the racehorses go.
I don't want no harping nor singing—
Such things with my style don't agree;
Where the hoofs of the horses are ringing
There's music sufficient for me.

And surely the thoroughbred horses
Will rise up again and begin
Fresh races on far-away courses,
And p'raps they might let me slip in.
It would look rather well the race-card on
'Mongst Cherubs and Seraphs and things,
'Angel Harrison's black gelding Pardon,
Blue halo, white body and wings.'

And if they have racing hereafter,
(And who is to say they will not?)
When the cheers and the shouting and laughter
Proclaim that the battle grows hot;
As they come down the racecourse a-steering,
He'll rush to the front, I believe;
And you'll hear the great multitude cheering
For Pardon, the son of Reprieve.

Uncle Bill

THE LARRIKIN'S LAMENT

My Uncle Bill! My Uncle Bill!
How doth my heart with anguish thrill!
For he, our chief, our Robin Hood,
Has gone to jail for stealing wood!
With tears and sobs my voice I raise
To celebrate my uncle's praise;
With all my strength, with all my skill,
I'll sing the song of Uncle Bill.

Convivial to the last degree,
An open-hearted sportsman he.
Did midnight howls our slumbers rob,
We said, 'It's uncle "on the job".'
When sounds of fight rang sharply out,
Then Bill was bound to be about,
The foremost figure in 'the scrap',
A terror to the local 'trap'.
To drink, or fight, or maim, or kill,
Came all alike to Uncle Bill.
And when he faced the music's squeak
At Central Court before the beak,
How carefully we sought our fob
To pay his fine of forty bob!
Recall the happy days of yore
When Uncle Bill went forth to war!
When all the street with strife was filled
And both the traps got nearly killed.
When the lone cabman on the stand
Was 'stoushed' by Bill's unaided hand,
And William mounted, filled with rum,
And drove the cab to kingdom come.
Remember, too, that famous fray
When the 'Black-reds', who hold their sway
O'er Surry Hills and Shepherd's Bush,
Descended on the 'Liver Push'.
Who cheered both parties long and loud?
Who heaved blue metal at the crowd!
And sooled his bulldog, Fighting Bet,
To bite, haphazard, all she met?
And when the mob were lodged in gaol
Who telegraphed to me for bail?
And—here I think he showed his sense—
Who calmly turned Queen's evidence?

Enough! I now must end my song,
My needless anguish, why prolong?
From what I've said, you'll own, I'm sure,
That Uncle Bill was pretty 'pure',
So, rowdies all, your glasses fill,
And—drink it standing—'Uncle Bill'.

The Corner-Man

I dreamt a dream at the midnight deep,
  When fancies come and go
To vex a man in his soothing sleep
  With thoughts of awful woe—
I dreamt that I was a corner-man
  Of a nigger minstrel show.

I cracked my jokes, and the building rang
  With laughter loud and long;
I hushed the house as I softly sang
  An old plantation song—
A tale of the wicked slavery days
  Of cruelty and wrong.

A small boy sat on the foremost seat—
  A mirthful youngster he;
He beat the time with his restless feet
  To each new melody,
And he picked me out as the brightest star
  Of the black fraternity.

'Oh father,' he said, 'what *would* we do
  If the corner-man should die?
I never saw such a man—did you?
  He makes the people cry,
And then, when he likes, he makes them laugh.'
  The old man made reply—

'We each of us fill a very small space
In the great creation's plan,
If a man don't keep his lead in the race
There's plenty more that can;
The world can very soon fill the place
Of even a corner-man.'

I woke with a jump, rejoiced to find
Myself at home in bed,
And I framed a moral in my mind
From the words the old man said.
The world will jog along just the same
When its corner-men are dead.

The corner-man was the singer and clown in a minstrel show.

'In re *a Gentleman, One*'

In Paterson's day when an attorney was called before the Court to answer for an alleged misconduct his name was not published until he was found guilty. The matter would appear in the papers as 'In re *a Gentleman, One of the Attorneys of the Supreme Court*', *or* 'In re *a Gent., One*'.

We see it each day in the paper,
And know that there's mischief in store;
That some unprofessional caper
Has landed a shark on the shore.
We know there'll be plenty of trouble
Before they get through with the fun,
Because he's been coming the double
On clients, has 'Gentleman, One'.

Alas for the gallant attorney,
Intent upon cutting a dash!
He starts on life's perilous journey
With rather more cunning than cash.
And fortune at first is inviting—
He struts his brief hour in the sun—
But, lo! on the wall is the writing
Of Nemesis, 'Gentleman, One'.

For soon he runs short of the dollars,
He fears he must go to the wall;
So Peter's trust-money he collars
To pay off his creditor, Paul;
Then robs right and left—for he goes it
In earnest when once he's begun.
Descensus averni—he knows it;
It's easy for 'Gentleman, One'.

The crash comes as sure as the seasons;
He loses his coin in a mine,
Or booming in land, or for reasons

Connected with women and wine.
Or maybe the cards or the horses
A share of the damage have done—
No matter; the end of the course is
The same: *'Re* a Gentleman, One.'

He struggles awhile to keep going,
To stave off detection and shame;
But creditors, clamorous growing,
Ere long put an end to the game.
At length the poor soldier of Satan
His course to a finish has run—
And just think of Windeyer waiting
To deal with 'A Gentleman, One'!

And some face it boldly, and brazen
The shame and the utter disgrace;
While others, more sensitive, hasten
Their names and their deeds to efface.
They snap the frail thread which the Furies
And Fates have so cruelly spun.
May the great Final Judge and His juries
Have mercy on 'Gentleman, One'!

How M'Ginnis Went Missing

Let us cease our idle chatter,
Let the tears bedew our cheek,
For a man from Tallangatta
Has been missing for a week.

Where the roaring flooded Murray
Covered all the lower land,
There he started in a hurry,
With a bottle in his hand.

And his fate is hid for ever,
But the public seem to think
That he slumbered by the river,
'Neath the influence of drink.

And they scarcely seem to wonder
That the river, wide and deep,
Never woke him with its thunder,
Never stirred him in his sleep.

As the crashing logs came sweeping,
And their tumult filled the air,
Then M'Ginnis murmured, sleeping,
' 'Tis a wake in ould Kildare.'

So the river rose and found him
Sleeping softly by the stream,
And the cruel waters drowned him
Ere he wakened from his dream.

And the blossom-tufted wattle,
Blooming brightly on the lea,
Saw M'Ginnis and the bottle
Going drifting out to sea.

Tar and Feathers

Oh, the circus swooped down
On the Narrabri town,
For the Narrabri populace moneyed are;
And the showman he smiled
At the folk he beguiled
To come all the distance from Gunnedah.

But a juvenile smart,
Who objected to 'part',
Went in 'on the nod', and to do it he
Crawled in through a crack
In the tent at the back,
For the boy had no slight ingenuity.

And says he with a grin,
'That's the way to get in;
But I reckon I'd better be quiet or
They'll spiflicate me,'
And he chuckled, for he
Had the loan of the circus proprietor.

But the showman astute
On that wily galoot
Soon dropped, and you'll say that he leathered him—
Not he; with a grim
Sort of humorous whim,
He took him and tarred him and feathered him.

Says he, 'You can go
Round the world with a show,
And knock every Injun and Arab wry;
With your name and your trade,
On the posters displayed,
The feathered what-is-it from Narrabri.'

Next day for his freak,
By a Narrabri beak,
He was jawed with a deal of verbosity;
For his only appeal
Was 'professional zeal'—
He wanted another monstrosity.

Said his worship, 'Begob!
You are fined forty bob,
And six shillin's costs to the clurk!' he says.
And the Narrabri joy,
Half bird and half boy,
Has a 'down' on himself and on circuses.

Mulligan's Mare

Oh, Mulligan's bar was the deuce of a place
To drink and to fight, and to gamble and race;
The height of choice spirits from near and from far
Were all concentrated on Mulligan's bar.

There was 'Jerry the Swell', and the jockey boy Ned,
'Dog-bite-me'—so called from the shape of his head—
And a man whom the boys, in their musical slang,
Designed as the 'Gaffer of Mulligan's Gang'.

Now, Mulligan's Gang had a racer to show,
A bad 'un to look at, a good 'un to go;
Whenever they backed her you safely might swear
She'd walk in a winner, would Mulligan's mare.

But Mulligan, having some radical views,
Neglected his business and got 'on the booze';
He took up with runners—a treacherous troop—
Who gave him away and he 'fell in the soup'.

And so it turned out on a fine summer day,
A bailiff turned up with a writ of *fi fa';*
He walked to the bar with a manner serene,
'I levy,' said he, 'in the name of the Queen.'

Then Mulligan wanted, in spite of the law,
To pay out the bailiff with '*one* on the jaw',
He drew out to hit him, but, ere you could wink,
He changed his intentions and stood him a drink.

A great consulation there straightaway befell
'Twixt jockey boy Neddy and Jerry the Swell,
And the man with the head, who remarked, 'Why,
you bet!
Dog-bite-me!' said he, 'but we'll diddle 'em yet.

'We'll slip out the mare from her stall in a crack,
And put in her place the old broken-down hack;
The hack is so like her, I'm ready to swear
The bailiff will think he has Mulligan's mare.

'So out with the racer and in with the screw,
We'll show him what Mulligan's talent can do;
And if he gets nasty and dares to say much
I'll knock him as stiff as my grandmother's crutch.'

Then off to the town went the mare and the lad;
The bailiff came out, never dream't he was 'had';
But marched to the stall with a confident air—
'I levy,' said he, 'upon Mulligan's mare.'

He never would let her go out of his sight,
He watched her by day and he watched her by
night,
For races were coming away in the west
And Mulligan's mare had a chance with the best.

And, thinking to quietly serve his own ends,
He sent off a wire to some bookmaking friends:
'Get all you can borrow, beg, snavel, or snare
And lay the whole lot against Mulligan's mare.'

The races came round, and a crowd on the course,
Were laying the mare till they made themselves
hoarse,
And Mulligan's party, with ardour intense,
They backed her for pounds and for shillings and
pence.

And think of the grief of the bookmaking host
At sound of the summons to go to the post—
For down to the start with her thoroughbred air
As fit as a fiddle pranced Mulligan's mare!

They started, and off went the boy to the front,
He cleared out at once, and he made it a hunt;
He steadied as rounding the corner they wheeled,
Then gave her her head and she smothered the field.

The race put her owner right clear of his debts,
He landed a fortune in stakes and in bets,
He paid the old bailiff the whole of his pelf,
And gave him a hiding to keep for himself.

So all you bold sportsmen take warning, I pray,
Keep clear of the running, you'll find it don't pay;
For the very best rule that you'll hear in a week—
Is never to bet on a thing that can speak.

And whether you're lucky or whether you lose,
Keep clear of the cards and keep clear of the booze,
And fortune in season will answer your prayer,
And send you a flyer like Mulligan's mare.

Clancy of The Overflow

I had written him a letter which I had, for want of better
Knowledge, sent to where I met him down the Lachlan, years ago;
He was shearing when I knew him, so I sent the letter to him,
Just 'on spec', addressed as follows: 'Clancy, of The Overflow'.

And an answer came directed in a writing unexpected,
(And I think the same was written with a thumbnail dipped in tar);
'Twas his shearing mate who wrote it, and *verbatim* I will quote it:
'Clancy's gone to Queensland droving, and we don't know where he are.'

* * *

In my wild erratic fancy visions come to me of Clancy
   Gone a-droving 'down the Cooper' where the Western drovers go;
As the stock are slowly stringing, Clancy rides behind them singing,
   For the drover's life has pleasures that the townsfolk never know.

And the bush hath friends to meet him, and their kindly voices greet him
   In the murmur of the breezes and the river on its bars,
And he sees the vision splendid of the sunlit plains extended,
   And at night the wondrous glory of the everlasting stars.

* * *

I am sitting in my dingy little office, where a stingy
   Ray of sunlight struggles feebly down between the houses tall,
And the foetid air and gritty of the dusty, dirty city
   Through the open window floating, spreads its foulness over all.

And in place of lowing cattle, I can hear the fiendish rattle
   Of the tramways and the buses making hurry down the street,
And the language uninviting of the gutter children fighting,
   Comes fitfully and faintly through the ceaseless tramp of feet.

And the hurrying people daunt me, and their pallid faces haunt me
   As they shoulder one another in their rush and nervous haste,
With their eager eyes and greedy, and their stunted forms and weedy,
   For townsfolk have no time to grow, they have no time to waste.

And I somehow rather fancy that I'd like to change with Clancy,
   Like to take a turn at droving where the seasons come and go,
While he faced the round eternal of the cashbook and the journal—
   But I doubt he'd suit the office, Clancy, of 'The Overflow'.

An Idyll of Dandaloo

On Western plains, where shade is not,
   'Neath summer skies of cloudless blue,
Where all is dry and all is hot,
   There stands the town of Dandaloo—
A township where life's total sum
Is sleep, diversified with rum.

Its grass-grown streets with dust are deep,
   'Twere vain endeavour to express
The dreamless silence of its sleep,
   Its wide, expansive drunkenness.
The yearly races mostly drew
A lively crowd to Dandaloo.

There came a sportsman from the East,
   The eastern land where sportsmen blow,
And brought with him a speedy beast—
   A speedy beast as horses go.
He came afar in hope to 'do'
The little town of Dandaloo.

Now this was weak of him, I wot—
  Exceeding weak, it seemed to me—
For we in Dandaloo were not
  The Jugginses we seemed to be;
In fact, we rather thought we knew
Our book by heart in Dandaloo.

We held a meeting at the bar,
  And met the question fair and square—
'We've stumped the country near and far
  To raise the cash for races here;
We've got a hundred pounds or two—
Not half so bad for Dandaloo.

'And now, it seems, we have to be
  Cleaned out by this here Sydney bloke,
With his imported horse; and he
  Will scoop the pool and leave us broke.
Shall we sit still, and make no fuss
While this chap climbs all over us?'

The races came to Dandaloo,
  And all the cornstalks from the West,
On ev'ry kind of moke and screw,
  Came forth in all their glory drest.
The stranger's horse, as hard as nails,
Look'd fit to run for New South Wales.

He won the race by half a length—
  Quite half a length, it seemed to me—
But Dandaloo, with all its strength,
  Roared out 'Dead heat!' most fervently;
And, after hesitation meet,
The judge's verdict was 'Dead heat!'

And many men there were could tell
  What gave the verdict extra force:
The stewards, and the judge as well—
  They all had backed the second horse.
For things like this they sometimes do
In larger towns than Dandaloo.

They ran it off; the stranger won,
  Hands down, by near a hundred yards
He smiled to think his troubles done;
  But Dandaloo held all the cards.
They went to scale and—cruel fate!—
His jockey turned out under-weight.

Perhaps they'd tampered with the scale!
  I cannot tell. I only know
It weighed him out all right. I fail
  To paint that Sydney sportsman's woe.
He said the stewards were a crew
Of low-lived thieves in Dandaloo.

He lifted up his voice, irate,
  And swore till all the air was blue;
So then we rose to vindicate
  The dignity of Dandaloo.
'Look here,' said we, 'you must not poke
Such oaths at us poor country folk.'

We rode him softly on a rail,
  We shied at him, in careless glee,
Some large tomatoes, rank and stale,
  And eggs of great antiquity—
Their wild, unholy fragrance flew
About the town of Dandaloo.

He left the town at break of day,
  He led his race-horse through the streets,
And now he tells the tale, they say,
  To every racing man he meets.
And Sydney sportsmen all eschew
The atmosphere of Dandaloo.

Song of the Future

'Tis strange that in a land so strong,
So strong and bold in mighty youth,
We have no poet's voice of truth
To sing for us a wondrous song.

Our chiefest singer yet has sung
In wild, sweet notes a passing strain,
All carelessly and sadly flung
To that dull world he thought so vain.

'I care for nothing, good nor bad,
My hopes are gone, my pleasures fled,
I am but sifting sand,' he said:
What wonder Gordon's songs were sad!

And yet, not always sad and hard;
In cheerful mood and light of heart
He told the tale of Britomarte,
And wrote the Rhyme of Joyous Guard.

And some have said that Nature's face
To us is always sad; but these
Have never felt the smiling grace
Of waving grass and forest trees
On sunlit plains as wide as seas.

'A land where dull Despair is king
O'er scentless flower and songless bird!'
But we have heard the bell-birds ring
Their silver bells at eventide,
Like fairies on the mountain side,
The sweetest note man ever heard.

The wild thrush lifts a note of mirth;
The bronze wing pigeons call and coo
Beside their nests the long day through;
The magpie warbles clear and strong
A joyous, glad, thanksgiving song,
For all God's mercies upon earth.

And many voices such as these
Are joyful sounds for those to tell,
Who know the Bush and love it well,
With all its hidden mysteries.

We cannot love the restless sea,
That rolls and tosses to and fro
Like some fierce creature in its glee;
For human weal or human woe
It has no touch of sympathy.

For us the bush is never sad:
Its myriad voices whisper low,
In tones the bushmen only know,
Its sympathy and welcome glad.

For us the roving breezes bring
From many a blossom-tufted tree—
Where wild bees murmur dreamily—
The honey-laden breath of Spring.

. . .

We have no tales of other days,
No bygone history to tell;
Our tales are told where camp-fires blaze
At midnight, when the solemn hush
Of that vast wonderland, the Bush,
Hath laid on every heart its spell.

Although we have no songs of strife,
Of bloodshed reddening the land,
We yet may find achievements grand
Within the bushman's quiet life.

Lift ye your faces to the sky
Ye far blue mountains of the West,
Who lie so peacefully at rest
Enshrouded in a haze of blue;
'Tis hard to feel that years went by

Before the pioneers broke through
Your rocky heights and walls of stone,
And made your secrets all their own.

For years the fertile Western plains
Were hid behind your sullen walls,
Your cliffs and crags and waterfalls
All weatherworn with tropic rains.

Between the mountains and the sea,
Like Israelites with staff in hand,
The people waited restlessly:
They looked towards the mountains old
And saw the sunsets come and go
With gorgeous golden afterglow,
That made the West a fairyland,
And marvelled what that West might be
Of which such wondrous tales were told.

For tales were told of inland seas
Like sullen oceans, salt and dead,
And sandy deserts, white and wan,
Where never trod the foot of man,
Nor bird went winging overhead,
Nor ever stirred a gracious breeze
To wake the silence with its breath—
A land of loneliness and death.

At length the hardy pioneers
By rock and crag found out the way,
And woke with voices of to-day
A silence kept for years and years.

Upon the Western slope they stood
And saw—a wide expanse of plain
As far as eye could stretch or see
Go rolling westward endlessly.
The native grasses, tall as grain,
Were waved and rippled in the breeze;
From boughs of blossom laden trees
The parrots answered back again.
They saw the land that it was good,
A land of fatness all untrod,
And gave their silent thanks to God.

The way is won! The way is won!
And straightway from the barren coast
There came a westward-marching host,
That aye and ever onward prest
With eager faces to the West,
Along the pathway of the sun.

The mountains saw them marching by:
They faced the all-consuming drought,
They would not rest in settled land:
But, taking each his life in hand,
Their faces ever westward bent
Beyond the farthest settlement,
Responding to the challenge cry
Of 'better country further out'.

And lo a miracle! the land
But yesterday was all unknown,
The wild man's boomerang was thrown
Where now great busy cities stand.
It was not much, you say, that these
Should win their way where none withstood;
In sooth there was not much of blood
No war was fought between the seas.

It was not much! but we who know
The strange capricious land they trod—
At times a stricken, parching sod,
At times with raging floods beset—
Through which they found their lonely way,
Are quite content that you should say
It was not much, while we can feel
That nothing in the ages old,
In song or story written yet
On Grecian urn or Roman arch,
Though it should ring with clash of steel,
Could braver histories unfold
Than this bush story, yet untold—
The story of their westward march.

But times are changed, and changes rung
From old to new—the olden days,
The old bush life and all its ways
Are passing from us all unsung.

The freedom, and the hopeful sense
Of toil that brought due recompense,
Of room for all, has passed away,
And lies forgotten with the dead.
Within our streets men cry for bread
In cities built but yesterday.

About us stretches wealth of land,
A boundless wealth of virgin soil
As yet unfruitful and untilled!
Our willing workmen, strong and skilled
Within our cities idle stand,
And cry aloud for leave to toil.

The stunted children come and go
In squalid lanes and alleys black;
We follow but the beaten track
Of other nations, and we grow
In wealth for some—for many, woe.

And it may be that we who live
In this new land apart, beyond
The hard old world grown fierce and fond
And bound by precedent and bond,
May read the riddle right and give
New hope to those who dimly see
That all things may be yet for good,
And teach the world at length to be
One vast united brotherhood.

* * *

So may it be! and he who sings
In accents hopeful, clear, and strong,
The glories which that future brings
Shall sing, indeed, a wond'rous song.

Our New Horse

The boys had come back from the races
  All silent and down on their luck;
They'd backed 'em, straight out and for places,
  But never a winner they struck.
They lost their good money on Slogan,
  And fell, most uncommonly flat,
When Partner, the pride of the Bogan,
  Was beaten by Aristocrat.

And one said, 'I move that instanter
  We sell out our horses and quit,
The brutes ought to win in a canter,
  Such trials they do when they're fit.
The last one they ran was a snorter—
  A gallop to gladden one's heart—
Two-twelve for a mile and a quarter,
  And finished as straight as a dart.

'And then when I think that they're ready
  To win me a nice little swag,
They are licked like the veriest neddy—
  They're licked from the fall of the flag.
The mare held her own to the stable,
  She died out to nothing at that,
And Partner he never seemed able
  To pace it with Aristocrat.

'And times have been bad, and the seasons
  Don't promise to be of the best;
In short, boys, there's plenty of reasons
  For giving the racing a rest.
The mare can be kept on the station—
  Her breeding is good as can be—
But Partner, his next destination
  Is rather a trouble to me.

'We can't sell him here, for they know him
  As well as the clerk of the course;
He's raced and won races till, blow him,
  He's done as a handicap horse.
A jady, uncertain performer,
  They weight him right out of the hunt,
And clap it on warmer and warmer
  Whenever he gets near the front.

'It's no use to paint him or dot him
  Or put any 'fake' on his brand,
For bushmen are smart, and they'd spot him
  In any sale-yard in the land.
The folk about here could all tell him,
  Could swear to each separate hair;
Let us send him to Sydney and sell him,
  There's plenty of Jugginses there.

'We'll call him a maiden, and treat 'em
  To trials will open their eyes,
We'll run their best horses and beat 'em
  And then won't they think him a prize.
I pity the fellow that buys him,
  He'll find in a very short space,
No matter how highly he tries him,
  The beggar won't race in a race.'

* * *

Next week, under 'Seller and Buyer',
  Appeared in the *Daily Gazette:*
'A racehorse for sale, and a flyer;
  Has never been started as yet;
A trial will show what his pace is;
  The buyer can get him in light,
And win all the handicap races.
  Apply here before Wednesday night.'

He sold for a hundred and thirty,
  Because of a gallop he had
One morning with Bluefish and Bertie,
  And donkey-licked both of 'em bad.
And when the old horse had departed,
  The life on the station grew tame;
The race-track was dull and deserted,
  The boys had gone back on the game.

The winter rolled by, and the station
Was green with the garland of spring
A spirit of glad exultation
Awoke in each animate thing.
And all the old love, the old longing,
Broke out in the breasts of the boys,
The visions of racing came thronging
With all its delirious joys.

The rushing of floods in their courses,
The rattle of rain on the roofs
Recalled the fierce rush of the horses,
The thunder of galloping hoofs.
And soon one broke out: 'I can suffer
No longer the life of a slug,
The man that don't race is a duffer,
Let's have one more run for the mug.

'Why, *everything* races, no matter
Whatever its method may be:
The waterfowl hold a regatta;
The possums run heats up a tree;
The emus are constantly sprinting
A handicap out on the plain;
It seems like all nature is hinting,
'Tis time to be at it again.

'The cockatoo parrots are talking
Of races to far away lands;
The native companions are walking
A go-as-you-please on the sands;
The little foals gallop for pastime;
The wallabies race down the gap;
Let's try it once more for the last time,
Bring out the old jacket and cap.

'And now for a horse; we might try one
Of those that are bred on the place,
But I think it better to buy one,
A horse that has proved he can race.
Let us send down to Sydney to Skinner,
A thorough good judge who can ride,
And ask him to buy us a spinner
To clean out the whole country-side.'

They wrote him a letter as follows:
'We want you to buy us a horse;
He must have the speed to catch swallows,
And stamina with it of course.
The price ain't a thing that'll grieve us,
It's getting a bad 'un annoys
The undersigned blokes, and believe us,
We're yours to a cinder, "the boys".'

He answered: 'I've bought you a hummer,
A horse that has never been raced;
I saw him run over the Drummer,
He held him outclassed and outpaced.
His breeding's not known, but they state he
Is born of a thoroughbred strain,
I paid them a hundred and eighty,
And started the horse in the train.'

They met him—alas, that these verses
Aren't up to the subject's demands—
Can't set forth their eloquent curses,
For Partner was back on their hands.
They went in to meet him in gladness,
They opened his box with delight—
A silent procession of sadness
They crept to the station at night.

And life has grown dull on the station,
The boys are all silent and slow;
Their work is a daily vexation,
And sport is unknown to them now.
Whenever they think how they stranded,
They squeal just like guinea-pigs squeal;
They bit their own hook, and were landed
With fifty pounds loss on the deal.

The Man from Snowy River

There was movement at the station, for the word had passed around
That the colt from old Regret had got away,
And had joined the wild bush horses—he was worth a thousand pound,
So all the cracks had gathered to the fray.
All the tried and noted riders from the stations near and far
Had mustered at the homestead overnight,
For the bushmen love hard riding where the wild bush horses are,
And the stock-horse snuffs the battle with delight.

There was Harrison, who made his pile when Pardon won the cup,
The old man with his hair as white as snow;
But few could ride beside him when his blood was fairly up—
He would go wherever horse and man could go.
And Clancy of the Overflow came down to lend a hand,

No better horseman ever held the reins;
For never horse could throw him while the saddle girths would stand,
He learnt to ride while droving on the plains.

And one was there, a stripling on a small and weedy beast,
He was something like a racehorse undersized,
With a touch of Timor pony—three parts thoroughbred at least—
And such as are by mountain horsemen prized.
He was hard and tough and wiry—just the sort that won't say die—
There was courage in his quick impatient tread;
And he bore the badge of gameness in his bright and fiery eye,
And the proud and lofty carriage of his head.

But so slight and weedy, one would doubt his power to stay,
And the old man said, 'That horse will never do
For a long and tiring gallop—lad, you'd better stop away,
Those hills are far too rough for such as you.'
So he waited sad and wistful—only Clancy stood his friend—
'I think we ought to let him come,' he said;
'I warrant he'll be with us when he's wanted at the end,
For both his horse and he are mountain bred.

'He hails from Snowy River, up by Kosciusko's side,
Where the hills are twice as steep and twice as rough,
Where a horse's hoofs strike firelight from the flint stones every stride,
The man that holds his own is good enough.
And the Snowy River riders on the mountains make their home,
Where the river runs those giant hills between;
I have seen full many horsemen since I first commenced to roam,
But nowhere yet such horsemen have I seen.'

So he went—they found the horses by the big mimosa clump—
They raced away towards the mountain's brow,
And the old man gave his orders, 'Boys, go at them from the jump,
No use to try for fancy riding now.
And, Clancy, you must wheel them, try and wheel them to the right.
Ride boldly, lad, and never fear the spills,
For never yet was rider that could keep the mob in sight,
If once they gain the shelter of those hills.'

So Clancy rode to wheel them—he was racing on the wing
Where the best and boldest riders take their place,
And he raced his stockhorse past them, and he made the ranges ring
With stockwhip, as he met them face to face.
Then they halted for a moment, while he swung the dreaded lash,

But they saw their well-loved mountain full in view,
And they charged beneath the stockwhip with a sharp and sudden dash,
And off into the mountain scrub they flew.

Then fast the horsemen followed, where the gorges deep and black
Resounded to the thunder of their tread,
And the stockwhips woke the echoes, and they fiercely answered back
From cliffs and crags that beetled overhead.
An upward, ever upward, the wild horses held their sway,
Where mountain ash and kurrajong grew wide;
And the old man muttered fiercely, 'We may bid the mob good day,
No man can hold them down the other side.'

When they reached the mountain's summit, even Clancy took a pull,
It well might make the boldest hold their breath,
The wild hop scrub grew thickly, and the hidden ground was full
Of wombat holes, and any slip was death.
But the man from Snowy River let the pony have his head,
And he swung his stockwhip round and gave a cheer,
And he raced him down the mountain like a torrent down its bed,
While the others stood and watched in very fear.

He sent the flint stones flying, but the pony kept his feet,
He cleared the fallen timbers in his stride,
And the man from Snowy River never shifted in his seat—
It was grand to see that mountain horseman ride.
Through the stringybarks and saplings, on the rough and broken ground,
Down the hillside at a racing pace he went;
And he never drew the bridle till he landed safe and sound,
At the bottom of that terrible descent.

He was right among the horses as they climbed the further hill
And the watchers on the mountain standing mute,
Saw him ply the stockwhip fiercely, he was right among them still,
As he raced across the clearing in pursuit.
Then they lost him for a moment, where two mountain gullies met
In the ranges, but a final glimpse reveals
On a dim and distant hillside the wild horses racing yet,
With the man from Snowy River at their heels.

And he ran them single-handed till their sides were white with foam.
He followed like a bloodhound in their track,
Till they halted cowed and beaten, then he turned their heads for home,
And alone and unassisted brought them back.
But his hardy mountain pony he could scarcely raise a trot,

He was blood from hip to shoulder from the spur;
But his pluck was still undaunted, and his courage fiery hot,
For never yet was mountain horse a cur.

And down by Kosciusko, where the pine-clad ridges raise
Their torn and rugged battlements on high,
Where the air is clear as crystal, and the white stars fairly blaze
At midnight in the cold and frosty sky,
And where around The Overflow the reed beds sweep and sway
To the breezes, and the rolling plains are wide,
The man from Snowy River is a household word today,
And the stockmen tell the story of his ride.

Gilhooley's Estate

Oh, Mr Gilhooley he turned up his toes,
As most of us do, soon or late;
And Jones was a lawyer, as everyone knows,
So they took him Gilhooley's Estate.

Gilhooley in life had been living so free
'Twas thought his possessions were great,
So Jones, with a smile, says, 'There's many a fee
For me in Gilhooley's Estate.'

They made out a list of his property fine,
It totalled a thousand-and-eight;
But the debts were nine-hundred-and-ninety-and nine—
The debts of Gilhooley's Estate.

So Mrs Gilhooley says, 'Jones, my dear man,
My childer have little to ait:
Just keep the expinses as low as you can
Against poor Gilhooley's Estate.'

But Jones says, 'The will isn't clear in its terms,
I fear it will need some debate,
And the law won't allow me (attorneys are worms)
To appear in Gilhooley's Estate.'

So a barrister-man, with a wig on his head
And a brief in his hand, quite elate,
Went up to the Court where they bury the dead,
Just to move in Gilhooley's Estate.

But his Honour the Judge said, 'I think that the joint
Legatees must be called to pro*bate*—
Ex parte Pokehorney is clear on the point—
The point of Gilhooley's Estate.

'I order a suit to be brought just to try
If this is correct that I state—
A nice friendly suit—and the costs by and by,
Must be borne by Gilhooley's Estate.'

So Mrs Gilhooley says, 'Jones, you'll appear!
Thim barristers' fees is too great;
The suit is but friendly.' 'Attorneys, my dear,
Can't be heard in Gilhooley's Estate.'

From the barristers' quarter a mighty hurrah
Arises both early and late:
It's only the whoop of the Junior Bar
Dividing Gilhooley's Estate.

Those Names

The shearers sat in the firelight, hearty and hale and strong
After the hard day's shearing, passing the joke along:
The 'ringer' that shore a hundred, as they never were shorn before,
And the novice who, toiling bravely, had tommy-hawked half a score,
The tarboy, the cook, and the slushy, the sweeper that swept the board,
The picker-up, and the penner, with the rest of the shearing horde.
There were men from the inland stations where the skies like a furnace glow,
And men from the Snowy River, the land of the frozen snow;
There were swarthy Queensland drovers who reckoned all land by miles,
And farmers' sons from the Murray, where many a vineyard smiles.
They started at telling stories when they wearied of cards and games,
And to give these stories a flavour they threw in some local names,
And a man from the bleak Monaro, away on the tableland,
He fixed his eyes on the ceiling, and he started to play his hand.

He told them of Adjintoothbong, where the pine-clad mountains freeze,
And the weight of the snow in summer breaks branches off the trees,
And, as he warmed to the business, he let them have it strong—
Nimitybelle, Conargo, Wheeo, Bongongolong;
He lingered over them fondly, because they recalled to mind
A thought of the old bush homestead, and the girl that he left behind.
Then the shearers all sat silent till a man in the corner rose;

Said he, 'I've travelled a-plenty but never heard names like those,
Out in the western districts, out on the Castlereagh
Most of the names are easy—short for a man to say.
'You've heard of Mungrybambone and the Gundabluey pine,
Quobbotha, Girilambone, and Terramungamine,
Quambone, Eunonyhareenyha, Wee Waa, and Buntijo—
'But the rest of the shearers stopped him: 'For the sake of your jaw, go slow,
If you reckon those names are short ones out where such names prevail,
Just try and remember some long ones before you begin the tale.'
And the man from the western district, though never a word he said,
Just winked with his dexter eyelid, and then he retired to bed.

Conroy's Gap

This was the way of it, don't you know—
Ryan was 'wanted' for stealing sheep,
And never a trooper, high or low,
Could find him—catch a weasel asleep!
Till Trooper Scott, from the Stockman's Ford—
A bushman, too, as I've heard them tell—
Chanced to find him drunk as a lord
Round at the Shadow of Death Hotel.

D' you know the place? It's a wayside inn,
A low grog-shanty—a bushman trap,
Hiding away in its shame and sin
Under the shelter of Conroy's Gap—
Under the shade of that frowning range,
The roughest crowd that ever drew breath—
Thieves and rowdies, uncouth and strange,
Were mustered round at the Shadow of Death.

The trooper knew that his man would slide
  Like a dingo pup, if he saw the chance;
And with half a start on the mountain side
  Ryan would lead him a merry dance.
Drunk as he was when the trooper came,
  To him that did not matter a rap—
Drunk or sober, he was the same,
  The boldest rider in Conroy's Gap.

'I want you, Ryan,' the trooper said,
  'And listen to me, if you dare resist,
So help me heaven, I'll shoot you dead!'
  He snapped the steel on his prisoner's wrist,
And Ryan, hearing the handcuffs click,
  Recovered his wits as they turned to go,
For fright will sober a man as quick
  As all the drugs that the doctors know.

There was a girl in that rough bar
  Went by the name of Kate Carew.
Quiet and shy as the bush girls are,
  But ready-witted and plucky, too.
She loved this Ryan, or so they say,
  And passing by, while her eyes were dim
With tears, she said in a careless way,
  'The Swagman's round in the stable, Jim.'

Spoken too low for the trooper's ear,
  Why should she care if he heard or not?
Plenty of swagmen far and near,
  And yet to Ryan it meant a lot.
That was the name of the grandest horse
  In all the district from east to west
In every show ring, on every course
  They always counted The Swagman best.

He was a wonder, a raking bay—
  One of the grand old Snowdon strain—
One of the sort that could race and stay
  With his mighty limbs and his length of rein.
Born and bred on the mountain side,
  He could race through scrub like a kangaroo,
The girl herself on his back might ride,
  And The Swagman would carry her safely
    through.

He would travel gaily from daylight's flush
  Till after the stars hung out their lamps,
There was never his like in the open bush,
  And never his match on the cattle-camps.
For faster horses might well be found
  On racing tracks, or a plain's extent,
But few, if any, on broken ground
  Could see the way that The Swagman went.

When this girl's father, old Jim Carew,
  Was droving out on the Castlereagh
With Conroy's cattle, a wire came through
  To say that his wife couldn't live the day.
And he was a hundred miles from home,
  As flies the crow, with never a track,
Through plains as pathless as ocean's foam,
  He mounted straight on The Swagman's back.

He left the camp by the sundown light,
  And the settlers out on the Marthaguy
Awoke and heard, in the dead of night,
  A single horseman hurrying by.
He crossed the Bogan at Dandaloo,
  And many a mile of the silent plain
That lonely rider behind him threw
  Before they settled to sleep again.

He rode all night and he steered his course
  By the shining stars with a bushman's skill,
And every time that he pressed his horse
  The Swagman answered him gamely still.
He neared his home as the east was bright,
  The doctor met him outside the town:
'Carew! How far did you come last night?'
  'A hundred miles since the sun went down.'

And his wife got round, and an oath he passed,
  So long as he or one of his breed
Could raise a coin, though it took their last
  The Swagman never should want a feed.
And Kate Carew, when her father died,
  She kept the horse and she kept him well:
The pride of the district far and wide,
  He lived in style at the bush hotel.

Such was The Swagman; and Ryan knew
   Nothing about could pace the crack;
Little he'd care for the man in blue
   If once he got on The Swagman's back.
But how to do it? A word let fall
   Gave him the hint as the girl passed by;
Nothing but 'Swagman—stable-wall;
   Go to the stable and mind your eye.'

He caught her meaning, and quickly turned
   To the trooper: 'Reckon you'll gain a stripe
By arresting me, and it's easily earned;
   Let's go to the stable and get my pipe,
The Swagman has it.' So off they went,
   And soon as ever they turned their backs
The girl slipped down, on some errand bent
   Behind the stable, and seized an axe.

The trooper stood at the stable door
   While Ryan went in quite cool and slow,
And then (the trick had been played before)
   The girl outside gave the wall a blow.
Three slabs fell out of the stable wall—
   'Twas done 'fore ever the trooper knew—
And Ryan, as soon as he saw them fall,
   Mounted The Swagman and rushed him through.

The trooper heard the hoof-beats ring
   In the stable yard, and he slammed the gate,
But The Swagman rose with a mighty spring
   At the fence, and the trooper fired too late,
As they raced away and his shots flew wide
   And Ryan no longer need care a rap,
For never a horse that was lapped in hide
   Could catch The Swagman in Conroy's Gap.

And that's the story. You want to know
   If Ryan came back to his Kate Carew;
Of course he should have, as stories go,
   But the worst of it is, this story's true:
And in real life it's a curtain rule,
   Whatever poets and authors say
Of high-toned robbers and all their school,
   These horsethief fellows aren't built that way.

Come back! Don't hope it—the slinking hound,
   He sloped across to the Queensland side,
And sold The Swagman for fifty pound,
   And stole the money, and more beside.
And took to drink, and by some good chance
   Was killed—thrown out of a stolen trap.
And that was the end of this small romance,
   The end of the story of Conroy's Gap.

On Kiley's Run

The roving breezes come and go
      On Kiley's Run,
The sleepy river murmurs low,
And far away one dimly sees
Beyond the stretch of forest trees—
Beyond the foothills dusk and dun—
The ranges sleeping in the sun
      On Kiley's Run.

'Tis many years since first I came
      To Kiley's Run,
More years than I would care to name
Since I, a stripling, used to ride
For miles and miles at Kiley's side,
The while in stirring tones he told
The stories of the days of old
      On Kiley's Run.

I see the old bush homestead now
On Kiley's Run,
Just nestled down beneath the brow
Of one small ridge above the sweep
Of river-flat, where willows weep
And jasmine flowers and roses bloom,
The air was laden with perfume
On Kiley's Run.

We lived the good old station life
On Kiley's Run,
With little thought of care or strife.
Old Kiley seldom used to roam,
He liked to make the Run his home,
The swagman never turned away
With empty hand at close of day
From Kiley's Run

We kept a racehorse now and then
On Kiley's Run,
And neighb'ring stations brought their men
To meetings where the sport was free,
And dainty ladies came to see
Their champions ride; with laugh and song
The old house rang the whole night long
On Kiley's Run.

The station hands were friends, I wot,
On Kiley's Run,
A reckless, merry-hearted lot—
All splendid riders, and they knew
The 'boss' was kindness through and through.
Old Kiley always stood their friend,
And so they served him to the end
On Kiley's Run.

But droughts and losses came apace
To Kiley's Run,
Till ruin stared him in the face;
He toiled and toiled while lived the light,
He dreamed of overdrafts at night:
At length, because he could not pay,
His bankers took the stock away
From Kiley's Run.

Old Kiley stood and saw them go
From Kiley's Run.
The well-bred cattle marching slow;
His stockmen, mates for many a day,
They wrung his hand and went away.
Too old to make another start,
Old Kiley died—of broken heart,
On Kiley's Run.

* * *

The owner lives in England now
Of Kiley's Run.
He knows a racehorse from a cow;
But that is all he knows of stock:
His chiefest care is how to dock
Expenses, and he sends from town
To cut the shearers' wages down
On Kiley's Run.

There are no neighbours anywhere
Near Kiley's Run.
The hospitable homes are bare,
The gardens gone; for no pretence
Must hinder cutting down expense:
The homestead that we held so dear
Contains a half-paid overseer
On Kiley's Run.

All life and sport and hope have died
On Kiley's Run.
No longer there the stockmen ride;
For sour-faced boundary riders creep
On mongrel horses after sheep,
Through ranges where, at racing speed,
Old Kiley used to 'wheel the lead'
On Kiley's Run.

There runs a lane for thirty miles
Through Kiley's Run.
On either side the herbage smiles,
But wretched trav'lling sheep must pass
Without a drink or blade of grass
Thro' that long lane of death and shame:
The weary drovers curse the name
Of Kiley's Run.

The name itself is changed of late
Of Kiley's Run.
They call it 'Chandos Park Estate'.
The lonely swagman through the dark
Must hump his swag past Chandos Park.
The name is English, don't you see,
The old name sweeter sounds to me
Of Kiley's Run

I cannot guess what fate will bring
To Kiley's Run
For chances come and changes ring
I scarcely think 'twill always be
Locked up to suit an absentee;
And if he lets it out in farms
His tenants soon will carry arms
On Kiley's Run

Come-by-Chance

As I pondered very weary o'er a volume long and dreary—
For the plot was void of interest—'twas that Postal Guide, in fact,
There I learnt the true location, distance, size, and population
Of each township, town, and village in the radius of the Act.

And I learnt that Puckawidgee stands beside the Murrumbidgee,
And that Booleroi and Bumble get their letters twice a year,
Also that the post inspector, when he visited Collector,
Closed the office up instanter, and re-opened Dungalear.

But my languid mood forsook me, when I found a name that took me,
Quite by chance I came across it—'Come-by-Chance' was what I read;
No location was assigned it, not a thing to help one find it,
Just an 'N' which stood for northward, and the rest was all unsaid.

I shall leave my home, and forthward wander stoutly to the northward
Till I come by chance across it, and I'll straightway settle down,
For there can't be any hurry, nor the slightest cause for worry
Where the telegraph don't reach you nor the railways run to town.

And one's letters and exchanges come by chance across the ranges,
Where a wiry young Australian leads a pack horse once a week,
And the good news grows by keeping, and you're spared the pain of weeping
Over bad news when the mailman drops the letters in the creek.

But I fear, and more's the pity, that there's really no such city,
For there's not a man can find it of the shrewdest folk I know,
'Come-by-Chance', be sure it never means a land of fierce endeavour,
It is just the careless country where the dreamers only go.

Though we work and toil and hustle in our life of haste and bustle,
All that makes our life worth living comes unstriven for and free;
Man may weary and importune, but the fickle goddess Fortune
Deals him out his pain or pleasure careless what his worth may be.

All the happy times entrancing, days of sport and nights of dancing,
Moonlit rides and stolen kisses, pouting lips and loving glance:
When you think of these be certain you have looked behind the curtain,
You have had the luck to linger just a while in 'Come-by-Chance'.

In the Droving Days

'Only a pound,' said the auctioneer,
'Only a pound; and I'm standing here
Selling this animal, gain or loss.
Only a pound for the drover's horse;
One of the sort that was never afraid,
One of the boys of the Old Brigade;
Thoroughly honest and game, I'll swear,
Only a little the worst for wear;
Plenty as bad to be seen in town,
Give me a bid and I'll knock him down;
Sold as he stands, and without recourse,
Give me a bid for the drover's horse.'

Loitering there in an aimless way
Somehow I noticed the poor old grey,
Weary and battered and screwed, of course,
Yet when I noticed the old grey horse,
The rough bush saddle, and single rein
Of the bridle laid on his tangled mane,
Straightway the crowd and the auctioneer
Seemed on a sudden to disappear,
Melted away in a kind of haze,
For my heart went back to the droving days.

Back to the road, and I crossed again
Over the miles of the saltbush plain—
The shining plain that is said to be
The dried-up bed of an inland sea,
Where the air so dry and so clear and bright
Refracts the sun with a wondrous light,
And out in the dim horizon makes
The deep blue gleam of the phantom lakes.

At dawn of day we would feel the breeze
That stirred the boughs of the sleeping trees,
And brought a breath of the fragrance rare
That comes and goes in that scented air;
For the trees and grass and the shrubs contain
A dry sweet scent on the saltbush plain.
For those that love it and understand,
The saltbush plain is a wonderland.
A wondrous country, where Nature's ways
Were revealed to me in the droving days.
We saw the fleet wild horses pass,
And the kangaroos through the Mitchell grass,
The emu ran with her frightened brood
All unmolested and unpursued.
But there rose a shout and a wild hubbub
When the dingo raced for his native scrub,
And he paid right dear for his stolen meals
With the drover's dogs at his wretched heels.
For we ran him down at a rattling pace,
While the packhorse joined in the stirring chase.
And a wild halloo at the kill we'd raise—
We were light of heart in the droving days.

'Twas a drover's horse, and my hand again
Made a move to close on a fancied rein.
For I felt the swing and the easy stride
Of the grand old horse that I used to ride

In drought or plenty, in good or ill,
That same old steed was my comrade still;
The old grey horse with his honest ways
Was a mate to me in the droving days.

When we kept watch in the cold and damp
If the cattle broke from the sleeping camp,
Over the flats and across the plain,
With my head bent down on my waving mane,
Through the boughs above and the stumps below
On the darkest night I would let him go
At a racing speed; he would choose his course,
And my life was safe with the old grey horse.
But man and horse had a favourite job,
When an outlaw broke from a station mob,
With a right good will was the stockwhip plied,
As the old horse raced at the straggler's side,
And the greenhide whip such a weal would raise,
We could use the whip in the droving days.

'Only a pound!' and this was the end—
Only a pound for the drover's friend.
The drover's friend that had seen this day,
And now was worthless, and cast away
With a broken knee and a broken heart
To be flogged and starved in a hawker's cart.
Well, I made a bid for a sense of shame
And the memories dear of the good old game.

'Thank you? Guinea! and cheap at that!
Against you there in the curly hat!
Only a guinea and one more chance,
Down he goes if there's no advance,
Third and the last time, one two! three!'
And the old grey horse was knocked down to me.
And now he's wandering fat and sleek,
On the lucerne flats by the Homestead Creek;
I dare not ride him for fear he'd fall,
But he does a journey to beat them all,
For though he scarcely a trot can raise,
He can take me back to the droving days.

The Flying Gang

A Song of the Railroad

I served my time, in the days gone by,
In the railway's clash and clang,
And I worked my way to the end, and I
Was the head of the 'Flying Gang'.
'Twas a chosen band that was kept at hand
In case of an urgent need,
Was it south or north we were started forth,
And away at our utmost speed.
If word reached town that a bridge was down,
The imperious summons rang—
'Come out with the pilot engine sharp,
And away with the flying gang.'
Then a piercing scream and a rush of steam
As the engine moved ahead,
With a measured beat by the slum and street
Of the busy town we fled,
By the uplands bright and the homesteads white,
With the rush of the western gale,
And the pilot swayed with the pace we made
As she rocked on the ringing rail.
And the country children clapped their hands
As the engine's echoes rang,
But their elders said: 'There is work ahead
When they send for the flying gang.'
Then across the miles of the saltbush plain
That gleamed with the morning dew,
Where the grasses waved like the ripening grain
The pilot engine flew,

A fiery rush in the open bush
Where the grade marks seemed to fly,
And the order sped on the wires ahead,
The pilot *must* go by.

The Governor's special must stand aside,
And the fast express go hang,
Let your orders be that the line is free
For the boys of the flying gang.

An Evening in Dandaloo

It was while we held our races—
Hurdles, sprints and steeplechases—
Up in Dandaloo,
That a crowd of Sydney stealers,
Jockeys, pugilists and spielers
Brought some horses, real heelers,
Came and put us through.

Beat our nags and won our money,
Made the game by no means funny,
Made us rather blue;
When the racing was concluded,
Of our hard-earned coin denuded
Dandaloonies sat and brooded
There in Dandaloo.

Night came down on Johnson's shanty
Where the grog was no way scanty,
And a tumult grew
Till some wild, excited person
Galloped down the township cursing,
'Sydney push have mobbed Macpherson,
Roll up, Dandaloo!'

Great St Denis! what commotion!
Like the rush of stormy ocean
Fiery horsemen flew.
Dust and smoke and din and rattle,
Down the street they spurred their cattle
To the war-cry of the battle,
'Wade in, Dandaloo!'

So the boys might have their fight out,
Johnson blew the bar-room light out,
Then, in haste, withdrew.
And in darkness and in doubting
Raged the conflict and the shouting,
'Give the Sydney push a clouting,
Go it, Dandaloo!'

Jack Macpherson seized a bucket,
Every head he saw he struck it—
Struck in earnest, too;
And a man from Lower Wattle,
Whom a shearer tried to throttle,
Hit out freely with a bottle

There in Dandaloo.
Skin and hair were flying thickly,
When a light was fetched, and quickly
Brought a fact to view—
On the scene of the diversion
Every single, solid person
Come along to help Macpherson—
All were Dandaloo!

When the list of slain was tabled—
Some were drunk and some disabled—
Still we found it true.
In the darkness and the smother
We'd been belting one another;
Jack Macpherson bashed his brother
There in Dandaloo.

So we drank, and all departed—
How the 'mobbing' yarn was started
No one ever knew—
And the stockmen tell the story
Of that conflict fierce and gory,
How we fought for love and glory
Up in Dandaloo.

It's a proverb now, or near it—
At the races you can hear it,
At the dog-fights, too!
Every shrieking, dancing drover
As the canines topple over
Yells applause to Grip or Rover,
'Give him "Dandaloo"!'

And the teamster slowly toiling
Through the deep black country, soiling
Wheels and axles, too,
Lays the whip on Spot and Banker,
Rouses Tarboy with a flanker—
'Redman! Ginger! Heave there! Yank her!
Wade in, Dandaloo!'

As Long as Your Eyes are Blue

'Will you love me, sweet, when my hair is grey
And my cheeks shall have lost their hue?
When the charms of youth shall have passed away
Will your love as of old prove true?

'For the looks may change, and the heart may range,
And the love be no longer fond;
Will you love with truth in the years of youth
And away to the years beyond?'

Oh, I love you, sweet, for your locks of brown
And the blush on your cheek that lies—
But I love you most for the kindly heart
That I see in your sweet blue eyes.

For the eyes are signs of the soul within,
Of the heart that is leal and true,
And, my own sweetheart, I shall love you still,
Just as long as your eyes are blue.

For the locks may bleach, and the cheeks of peach
May be reft of the golden hue;
But, my own sweetheart, I shall love you still,
Just as long as your eyes are blue.

Been There Before

There came a stranger to Walgett town,
To Walgett town when the sun was low,
And he carried a thirst that was worth a crown,
Yet how to quench it he did not know;
But he thought he might take those yokels down,
The guileless yokels of Walgett town.

They made him a bet in a private bar,
In a private bar when the talk was high,
And they bet him some pounds no matter how far
He could pelt a stone, yet he could not shy
A stone right over the river so brown,
The Darling river at Walgett town.

He knew that the river from bank to bank
Was fifty yards, and he smiled a smile
As he trundled down, but his hopes they sank
For there wasn't a stone within fifty mile;
For the saltbush plain and the open down
Produce no quarries in Walgett town.

The yokels laughed at his hopes o'erthrown,
And he stood awhile like a man in a dream;
Then out of his pocket he fetched a stone,
And pelted it over the silent stream—
He had been there before: he had wandered down
On a previous visit to Walgett town.

A Mountain Station

I bought a run a while ago,
On country rough and ridgy,
Where wallaroos and wombats grow—
The Upper Murrumbidgee.
The grass is rather scant, it's true,
But this a fair exchange is,
The sheep can see a lovely view
By climbing up the ranges.

And 'She-oak Flat' 's the station's name,
I'm not surprised at that, sirs:
The oaks were there before I came,
And I supplied the flat, sirs.
A man would wonder how it's done,
The stock so soon decreases—
They sometimes tumble off the run
And break themselves to pieces.

I've tried to make expenses meet,
But wasted all my labours,
The sheep the dingoes didn't eat
Were stolen by the neighbours.
They stole my pears—my native pears—
Those thrice-convicted felons,
And ravished from me unawares
My crop of paddymelons.

And sometimes under sunny skies,
Without an explanation,
The Murrumbidgee used to rise
And overflow the station.
But this was caused (as now I know)
When summer sunshine glowing
Had melted all Kiandra's snow
And set the river going.

And in the news, perhaps you read:
 'Stock passings. Puckawidgee,
Fat cattle: Seven hundred head
 Swept down the Murrumbidgee;
Their destination's quite obscure,
 But somehow, there's a notion,
Unless the river falls, they're sure
 To reach the Southern Ocean.'

So after that I'll give it best;
 No more with Fate I'll battle.
I'll let the river take the rest,
 For those were all my cattle.
And with one comprehensive curse
 I close my brief narration,
And advertise it in my verse—
 'For Sale! A Mountain Station.'

The Open Steeplechase

I had ridden over hurdles up the country once or twice,
By the side of Snowy River with a horse they called 'The Ace'.
And we brought him down to Sydney, and our rider Jimmy Rice,
Got a fall and broke his shoulder, so they nabbed me in a trice—
Me, that never wore the colours, for the Open Steeplechase.

'Make the running,' said the trainer, 'it's your only chance whatever,
Make it hot from start to finish, for the old black horse can stay,
And just think of how they'll take it, when they hear on Snowy River
That the country boy was plucky, and the country horse was clever
You must ride for old Monaro and the mountain boys to-day.'

'Are you ready?' said the starter, as we held the horses back.
All ablazing with impatience, with excitement all aglow;
Before us like a ribbon stretched the steeplechasing track,
And the sun-rays glistened brightly on the chestnut and the black
As the starter's words came slowly, 'Are—you—ready? Go!'

Well, I scarcely knew we'd started, I was stupid-like with wonder
Till the field closed up beside me and a jump appeared ahead.
And we flew it like a hurdle, not a baulk and not a blunder,
As we charged it all together, and it fairly whistled under,
And then some were pulled behind me and a few shot out and led.

So we ran for half the distance, and I'm making no pretences
When I tell you I was feeling very nervous-like and queer,
For those jockeys rode like demons; you would think they'd lost their senses
If you saw them rush their horses at those rasping five-foot fences—
And in place of making running I was falling to the rear.

Till a chap came racing past me on a horse they called 'The Quiver',
And said he, 'My country joker, are you going to give it best?
Are you frightened of the fences? does their stoutness make you shiver?
Have they come to breeding cowards by the side of Snowy River?
Are there riders on Monaro?—' but I never heard the rest.

For I drove The Ace and sent him just as fast as he could pace it,
At the big black line of timber stretching fair across the track,
And he shot beside The Quiver. 'Now,' said I, 'my boy, we'll race it.
You can come with Snowy River if you're only game to face it;
Let us mend the pace a little and we'll see who cries a crack.'

So we raced away together, and we left the others standing,
And the people cheered and shouted as we settled down to ride,
And we clung beside The Quiver. At his taking off and landing
I could see his scarlet nostril and his mighty ribs expanding,
And The Ace stretched out in earnest and we held him stride for stride.

But the pace was so terrific that they soon ran out their tether—
They were rolling in their gallop, they were fairly blown and beat—
But they both were game as pebbles—neither one would show the feather.
And we rushed them at the fences, and they cleared them both together,
Nearly every time they clouted, but they somehow kept their feet.

Then the last jump rose before us, and they faced it game as ever—
We were both at spur and whipcord, fetching blood at every bound—
And above the people's cheering and the cries of 'Ace' and 'Quiver',
I could hear the trainer shouting, 'One more run for Snowy River.'
Then we struck the jump together and came smashing to the ground.

Well, The Quiver ran to blazes, but The Ace stood still and waited,
Stood and waited like a statue while I scrambled on his back.
There was no one next or near me for the field was fairly slated,
So I cantered home a winner with my shoulder dislocated,
While the man that rode The Quiver followed limping down the track.

And he shook my hand and told me that in all his days he never
Met a man who rode more gamely, and our last set to was prime,
And we wired them on Monaro how we chanced to beat The Quiver.
And they sent us back an answer, 'Good old sort from Snowy River:
Send us word each race you start in and we'll back you every time.'

The Pannikin Poet

There's nothing here sublime,
But just a roving rhyme?
Run off to pass the time,
With nought titanic in
The theme that it supports,
And, though it treats of quarts,
It's bare of golden thoughts
It's just a pannikin.

I think it's rather hard
That each Australian bard—
Each wan, poetic card—
With thoughts galvanic in
His fiery soul alight,
In wild aerial flight,
Will sit him down and write
About a pannikin.

He makes some new chum fare
From out his English lair
To hunt the native bear,
That curious mannikin;
And then when times get bad
That wondering English lad
Writes out a message sad
Upon his pannikin:

'O mother, think of me
Beneath the wattle tree'
(For you may bet that he
Will drag the wattle in)
'O mother, here I think
That I shall have to sink,
There ain't a single drink
The water-bottle in.'

The dingo homeward hies,
The sooty crows uprise
And caw their fierce surprise
A tone Satanic in;
And bearded bushmen tread
Around the sleeper's head—
'See here—the bloke is dead!
Now where's his pannikin?'

They read his words and weep,
And lay him down to sleep
Where wattle-branches sweep,
A style mechanic in;
And, reader, that's the way
The poets of to-day
Spin out their little lay
About a pannikin.

In Defence of the Bush

So you're back from up the country, Mister Lawson, where you went,
And you're cursing all the business in a bitter discontent;
Well, we grieve to disappoint you, and it makes us sad to hear
That it wasn't cool and shady—and there wasn't plenty beer,
And the loony bullock snorted when you first came into view;
Well, you know it's not so often that he sees a swell like you;
And the roads were hot and dusty, and the plains were burnt and brown,
And no doubt you're better suited drinking lemon squash in town.

Yet, perchance, if you should journey down the very track you went
In a month or two at furthest you would wonder what it meant,
Where the sunbaked earth was gasping like a creature in its pain
You would find the grasses waving like a field of summer grain,
And the miles of thirsty gutters blocked with sand and choked with mud,
You would find them mighty rivers with a turbid, sweeping flood;
For the rain and drought and sunshine make no changes in the street,
In the sullen line of buildings and the ceaseless tramp of feet;
But the bush hath moods and changes, as the seasons rise and fall,
And the men who know the bush-land—they are loyal through it all.

But you found the bush was dismal and a land of no delight,
Did you chance to hear a chorus in the shearers' huts at night?
Did they 'rise up, William Riley' by the camp-fire's cheery blaze?
Did they rise him as we rose him in the good old droving days?
And the women of the homesteads and the men you chanced to meet
Were their faces sour and saddened like the 'faces in the street',
And the 'shy selector children'—were they better now or worse
Than the little city urchins who would greet you with a curse?
Is not such a life much better than the squalid street and square
Where the fallen women flaunt it in the fierce electric glare,
Where the sempstress plies her sewing till her eyes are sore and red
In a filthy, dirty attic toiling on for daily bread?
Did you hear no sweeter voices in the music of the bush
Than the roar of trams and 'buses, and the war-whoop of 'the push'?
Did the magpies rouse your slumbers with their carol sweet and strange?
Did you hear the silver chiming of the bell-birds on the range?
But, perchance, the wild birds' music by your senses was despised,
For you say you'll stay in townships till the bush is civilised.

Would you make it a tea-garden and on Sundays have a band
Where the 'blokes' might take their 'donahs', with a 'public' close at hand?
You had better stick to Sydney and make merry with the 'push',
For the bush will never suit you, and you'll never suit the bush.

An Answer to Various Bards

Well, I've waited mighty patient while they all came rolling in,
Mister Lawson, Mister Dyson, and the others of their kin,
With their dreadful, dismal stories of the Overlander's camp,
How his fire is always smoky, and his boots are always damp;
And they paint it so terrific it would fill one's soul with gloom—
But you know they're fond of writing about 'corpses' and 'the tomb'.
So, before they curse the bushland, they should let their fancy range,
And take something for their livers, and be cheerful for a change.

Now, for instance, Mister Lawson—well, of course, we almost cried
At the sorrowful description how his 'little 'Arvie' died,
And we lachrymosed in silence when 'His Father's Mate' was slain;
Then he went and killed the father, and we had to weep again.
Ben Duggan and Jack Denver, too, he caused them to expire,
After which he cooked the gander of Jack Dunn, of Nevertire;
And, no doubt, the bush is wretched if you judge it by the groan
Of the sad and soulful poet with a graveyard of his own.

And he spoke in terms prophetic of a revolution's heat,
When the world should hear the clamour of those people in the street;
But the shearer chaps who start it—why, he rounds on them in blame,
And he calls 'em 'agitators who are living on the game'.
But I 'over-write' the bushmen! Well, I own without a doubt
That I always see a hero in the 'man from furthest out'.
I could never contemplate him through an atmosphere of gloom,
And a bushman never struck me as a subject for 'the tomb'.

If it ain't all 'golden sunshine' where the 'wattle branches wave',
Well, it ain't all damp and dismal, and it ain't all 'lonely grave'.
And, of course, there's no denying that the bushman's life is rough,
But a man can easy stand it if he's built of sterling stuff;
Though it's seldom that the drover gets a bed of eiderdown,
Yet the man who's born a bushman, he gets mighty sick of town,
For he's jotting down the figures, and he's adding up the bills
While his heart is simply aching for a sight of Southern hills.

Then he hears a wool-team passing with a rumble and a lurch,
And, although the work is pressing, yet it brings him off his perch.
For it stirs him like a message from his station friends afar
And he seems to sniff the ranges in the scent of wool and tar;
And it takes him back in fancy, half in laughter, half in tears,
To a sound of other voices and a thought of other years,
When the woolshed rang with bustle from the dawning of the day,
And the shear-blades were a-clicking to the cry of 'Wool away!'

Then his face was somewhat browner, and his frame was firmer set—
And he feels his flabby muscles with a feeling of regret.
But the wool-team slowly passes, and his eyes go sadly back
To the dusty little table and the papers in the rack,
And his thoughts go to the terrace where his sickly children squall,
And he thinks there's something healthy in the bush-life after all.
But we'll go no more a-droving in the wind or in the sun,
For our fathers' hearts have failed us, and the droving days are done.

There's a nasty dash of danger where the long-horned bullock wheels,
And we like to live in comfort and to get our reg'lar meals.
For to hang around the townships suits us better, you'll agree,
And a job at washing bottles is the job for such as we.
Let us herd into the cities, let us crush and crowd and push
Till we lose the love of roving, and we learn to hate the bush;
And we'll turn our aspirations to a city life and beer,
And we'll slip across to England—it's a nicer place than here.
For there's not much risk of hardship where all comforts are in store,
And the theatres are in plenty, and the pubs are more and more.
But that ends it, Mister Lawson, and it's time to say good-bye,
So we must agree to differ in all friendship, you and I.
Yes, we'll work our own salvation with the stoutest hearts we may,
And if fortune only favours we will take the road some day,
And go droving down the river 'neath the sunshine and the stars,
And then return to Sydney and vermilionize the bars.

The Boss of the Admiral Lynch

Did you ever hear tell of Chili? I was readin' the other day
Of President Balmaceda and of how he was sent away.
It seems that he didn't suit 'em—they thought that they'd like a change,
So they started an insurrection and chased him across the range.
They seemed to be restless people—and, judging by what you hear,
They raise up these revolutions 'bout two or three times a year;
And the man that goes out of office, he goes for the boundary *quick,*
For there isn't no vote by ballot—it's bullets that does the trick.
And it ain't like a real battle, where the prisoners' lives are spared,
And they fight till there's one side beaten and then there's a truce declared.

And the man that has got the licking goes down like a blooming lord
To hand in his resignation and give up his blooming sword,
And the other man bows and takes it, and everything's all polite—
This wasn't that kind of a picnic, this wasn't that sort of a fight.
For the pris'ners they took—they shot 'em; no odds were they small or great,
If they'd collared old Balmaceda, they reckoned to shoot him straight.
A lot of bloodthirsty devils they were—but there ain't a doubt
They must have been real plucked 'uns—the way that they fought it out,
And the king of 'em all, I reckon, the man that could stand a pinch,
Was the boss of a one-horse gunboat. They called her the *Admiral Lynch.*

Well, he was for Balmaceda, and after the war was done,
And Balmaceda was beaten and his troops had been forced to run,
The other man fetched his army and proceeded to do things brown,
He marched 'em into the fortress and took command of the town.
Cannon and guns and horses troopin' along the road,
Rumblin' over the bridges, and never a foeman showed
Till they came in sight of the harbour, and the very first thing they see
Was this mite of a one-horse gunboat a-lying against the quay,
And there as they watched they noticed a flutter of crimson rag,
And under their eyes he hoisted old Balmaceda's flag.

Well, I tell you it fairly knocked 'em—it just took away their breath,
For he must ha' known if they caught him, 'twas nothin' but sudden death.
An' he'd got no fire in his furnace, no chance to put out to sea,
So he stood by his gun and waited with his vessel against the quay.
Well, they sent him a civil message to say that the war was done,
And most of his side were corpses, and all that were left had run;
And blood had been spilt sufficient, so they gave him a chance to decide
If he'd haul down his bit of bunting and come on the winning side.
He listened and heard their message, and answered them all polite,

That he was a Spanish hidalgo, and the men of his race *must* fight!
A gunboat against an army, and with never a chance to run,
And them with their hundred cannon and him with a single gun:
The odds were a trifle heavy—but he wasn't the sort to flinch,
So he opened fire on the army, did the boss of the *Admiral Lynch.*

They pounded his boat to pieces, they silenced his single gun,
And captured the whole consignment, for none of 'em cared to run;
And it don't say whether they shot him—it don't even give his name—
But whatever they did I'll wager that he went to his graveyard game.
I tell you those old hidalgos so stately and so polite,
They turn out the real Maginnis when it comes to an uphill fight.
There was General Alcantara, who died in the heaviest brunt,
And General Alzereca was killed in the battle's front;
But the king of 'em all, I reckon—the man that could stand a pinch—
Was the man who attacked the army with the gunboat *Admiral Lynch.*

The Man from Ironbark

It was the man from Ironbark who struck the Sydney town,
He wandered over street and park, he wandered up and down.
He loitered here, he loitered there, till he was like to drop,
Until at last in sheer despair he sought a barber's shop.
' 'Ere! shave my beard and whiskers off, I'll be a man of mark,
I'll go and do the Sydney toff up home in Ironbark.'

The barber man was small and flash, as barbers mostly are,
He wore a strike-your-fancy sash, he smoked a huge cigar:
He was a humorist of note and keen at repartee,
He laid the odds and kept a 'tote', whatever that may be,
And when he saw our friend arrive, he whispered 'Here's a lark!
Just watch me catch him all alive, this man from Ironbark.'

There were some gilded youths that sat along the barber's wall.
Their eyes were dull, their heads were flat, they had no brains at all;
To them the barber passed the wink, his dexter eyelid shut,
'I'll make this bloomin' yokel think his bloomin' throat is cut.'
And as he soaped and rubbed it in he made a rude remark:
'I s'pose the flats is pretty green up there in Ironbark.'

A grunt was all reply he got; he shaved the bushman's chin,
Then made the water boiling hot and dipped the razor in.
He raised his hand, his brow grew black, he paused awhile to gloat,
Then slashed the red-hot razor-back across his victim's throat;
Upon the newly-shaven skin it made a livid mark—
No doubt it fairly took him in—the man from Ironbark.

He fetched a wild up-country yell might wake the dead to hear,
And though his throat, he knew full well, was cut from ear to ear,
He struggled gamely to his feet, and faced the murd'rous foe:
'You've done for me! you dog, I'm beat! one hit before I go!
I only wish I had a knife, you blessed murdering shark!
But you'll remember all your life, the man from Ironbark.'

He lifted up his hairy paw, with one tremendous clout
He landed on the barber's jaw, and knocked the barber out.
He set to work with tooth and nail, he made the place a wreck;
He grabbed the nearest gilded youth, and tried to break his neck.
And all the while his throat he held to save his vital spark,
And 'Murder! Bloody Murder!' yelled the man from Ironbark.

A peeler man who heard the din came in to see the show;
He tried to run the bushman in, but he refused to go.
And when at last the barber spoke, and said ' 'Twas all in fun—
' 'Twas just a little harmless joke, a trifle overdone.'
'A joke!' he cried, 'By George, that's fine; a lively sort of lark;
I'd like to catch that murdering swine some night in Ironbark.'

And now while round the shearing floor the list'ning shearers gape,
He tells the story o'er and o'er, and brags of his escape.
'Them barber chaps what keeps a tote, By George, I've had enough.
One tried to cut my bloomin' throat, but thank the Lord it's tough.'
And whether he's believed or no, there's one thing to remark,
That flowing beards are all the go way up in Ironbark.

A Bushman's Song

I'm travellin' down the Castlereagh, and I'm a station hand,
I'm handy with the ropin' pole, I'm handy with the brand,
And I can ride a rowdy colt, or swing the axe all day,
But there's no demand for a station hand along the Castlereagh.

So it's shift, boys, shift, for there isn't the slightest doubt
That we've got to make a shift to the stations further out
With the packhorse runnin' after, for he follows like a dog,
We must strike across the country at the old jig-jog.

This old black horse I'm riding—if you'll notice what's his brand,
He wears the crooked R, you see—none better in the land.
He takes a lot of beating', and the other day we tried,
For a bit of a joke, with a racing bloke, for twenty pounds aside.

It was shift, boys, shift, for there wasn't the slightest doubt,
That I had to make him shift, for the money was nearly out;
But he cantered home a winner, with the other one at the flog—
He's a red-hot sort to pick up with his old jig-jog.

I asked a cove for shearin' once along the Marthaguy:
'We shear non-union here,' says he. 'I call it scab,' says I.
I looked along the shearin' floor before I turned to go—
There were eight or ten dashed Chinamen a-shearin' in a row.

It was shift, boys, shift, for there wasn't the slightest doubt
It was time to make a shift with the leprosy about.
So I saddled up my horses, and I whistled to my dog,
And I left his scabby station at the old jig-jog.

I went to Illawarra where my brother's got a farm,
He has to ask his landlord's leave before he lifts his arm;
The landlord owns the countryside—man, woman, dog, and cat,
They haven't the cheek to dare to speak without they touch their hat.

It was shift, boys, shift, for there wasn't the slightest doubt
Their little landlord god and I would soon have fallen out;
Was I to touch my hat to him?—was I his bloomin' dog?
So I makes for up the country at the old jig-jog.

But it's time that I was movin', I've a mighty way to go
Till I drink artesian water from a thousand feet below;

Till I meet the overlanders with the cattle comin' down,
And I'll work a while till I make a pile, then have a spree in town.

So, it's shift, boys, shift, for there isn't the slightest doubt
We've got to make a shift to the stations further out;
The packhorse runs behind us, for he follows like a dog,
And we cross a lot of country at the old jig-jog.

The Geebung Polo Club

It was somewhere up the country, in a land of rock and scrub,
That they formed an institution called the Geebung Polo Club.
They were long and wiry natives from the rugged mountain side,
And the horse was never saddled that the Geebungs couldn't ride;
But their style of playing polo was irregular and rash—
They had mighty little science, but a mighty lot of dash:
And they played on mountain ponies that were muscular and strong,
Though their coats were quite unpolished, and their manes and tails were long.
And they used to train those ponies wheeling cattle in the scrub:
They were demons, were the members of the Geebung Polo Club.

It was somewhere down the country, in a city's smoke and steam,
That a polo club existed, called 'The Cuff and Collar Team'.
As a social institution 'twas a marvellous success,
For the members were distinguished by exclusiveness and dress.
They had natty little ponies that were nice, and smooth, and sleek,
For their cultivated owners only rode 'em once a week.
So they started up the country in pursuit of sport and fame,
For they meant to show the Geebungs how they ought to play the game;
And they took their valets with them—just to give their boots a rub
Ere they started operations on the Geebung Polo Club.

Now my readers can imagine how the contest ebbed and flowed,
When the Geebung boys got going it was time to clear the road;
And the game was so terriffic that ere half the time was gone
A spectator's leg was broken—just from merely looking on.
For they waddied one another till the plain was strewn with dead,
While the score was kept so even that they neither got ahead.
And the Cuff and Collar Captain, when he tumbled off to die,
Was the last surviving player—so the game was called a tie.
Then the Captain of the Geebungs raised him slowly from the ground,
Though his wounds were mostly mortal, yet he fiercely gazed around;
There was no one to oppose him—all the rest were in a trance,

So he scrambled on his pony for his last expiring chance,
For he meant to make an effort to get victory to his side;
So he struck at goal—and missed it—then he tumbled off and died.

By the old Campaspe River, where the breezes shake the grass,
There's a row of little gravestones that the stockmen never pass,
For they bear a crude inscription saying, 'Stranger, drop a tear,
For the Cuff and Collar players and the Geebung boys lie here.'
And on misty moonlit evenings, while the dingoes howl around,
You can see their shadows flitting down that phantom polo ground;
You can hear the loud collisions as the flying players meet,
And the rattle of the mallets, and the rush of ponies' feet,
Till the terrified spectator rides like blazes to the pub—
He's been haunted by the spectres of the Geebung Polo Club.

When Dacey Rode the Mule

'Twas to a small, up-country town,
When we were boys at school,
There came a circus with a clown,
Likewise a bucking mule.
The clown announced a scheme they had
Spectators for to bring—
They'd give a crown to any lad
Who'd ride him round the ring.

And, gentle reader, do not scoff
Nor think a man a fool—
To buck a porous-plaster off
Was pastime to that mule.

The boys got on; he bucked like sin;
He threw them in the dirt.
What time the clown would raise a grin
By asking, 'Are you hurt?'
But Johnny Dacey came one night,
The crack of all the school;
Said he, 'I'll win the crown all right;
Bring in your bucking mule.'

The elephant went off his trunk,
The monkey played the fool,
And all the band got blazing drunk
When Dacey rode the mule.

But soon there rose a galling shout
Of laughter, for the clown
From somewhere in his pants drew out
A little paper crown.
He placed the crown on Dacey's head
While Dacey looked a fool;
'Now, there's your crown, my lad,' he said,
'For riding of the mule!'

The band struck up with 'Killaloe',
And 'Rule Britannia, Rule',
And 'Young Man from the Country', too,
When Dacey rode the mule.

Then Dacey, in a furious rage,
For vengeance on the show
Ascended to the monkeys' cage
And let the monkeys go;
The blue-tailed ape and chimpanzee
He turned abroad to roam;
Good faith! It was a sight to see
The people step for home.

For big baboons with canine snout
Are spiteful, as a rule—
The people didn't sit it out,
When Dacey rode the mule.

And from the beasts he let escape,
The bushmen all declare,
Were born some creatures partly ape
And partly native-bear.
They're rather few and far between,
The race is nearly spent;
But some of them may still be seen
In Sydney Parliament.

And when those legislators fight,
And drink, and act the fool,
Just blame it on that torrid night
When Dacey rode the mule.

Black Swans

As I lie at rest on a patch of clover
In the Western Park when the day is done,
I watch as the wild black swans fly over
With their phalanx turned to the sinking sun;
And I hear the clang of their leader crying
To a lagging mate in the rearward flying,
And they fade away in the darkness dying,
Where the stars are mustering one by one

Oh! ye wild black swans, 'twere a world of wonder
For a while to join in your westward flight,
With the stars above and the dim earth under,
Through the cooling air of the glorious night.
As we swept along on our pinions winging,
We should catch the chime of a church-bell ringing,
Or the distant note of a torrent singing,
Or the far-off flash of a station light.

From the northern lakes with the reeds and rushes,
Where the hills are clothed with purple haze,
Where the bell-birds chime and the songs of thrushes
Make music sweet in the jungle maze,
They will hold their course to the westward ever,
Till they reach the banks of the old grey river,
Where the waters wash, and the reed-beds quiver
In the burning heat of the summer days.
Oh! ye strange wild birds, will ye bear a greeting
To the folk that live in that western land?
Then for every sweep of your pinions beating,
Ye shall bear a wish to the sunburnt band,
To the stalwart men who are stoutly fighting
With the heat and drought and the dust-storm smiting,
Yet whose life somehow has a strange inviting,
When once to the work they have put their hand.

Facing it yet! Oh, my friend stout-hearted,
What does it matter for rain or shine,
For the hopes deferred and the gain departed?
Nothing could conquer that heart of thine.
And thy health and strength are beyond confessing
As the only joys that are worth possessing.
May the days to come be as rich in blessing
As the days we spent in the auld lang syne.

I would fain go back to the old grey river,
To the old bush days when our hearts were light,
But, alas! those days they have fled for ever,
They are like the swans that have swept from sight.
And I know full well that the strangers' faces
Would meet us now in our dearest places;
For our day is dead and has left no traces
But the thoughts that live in my mind to-night.
There are folk long dead, and our hearts would
sicken—

We would grieve for them with a bitter pain,
If the past could live and the dead could quicken,
We then might turn to that life again.
But on lonely nights we would hear them calling,
We should hear their steps on the pathways falling,
We should loathe the life with a hate appalling
In our lonely rides by the ridge and plain.

*　　*　　*

In the silent park is a scent of clover,
And the distant roar of the town is dead,
And I hear once more as the swans fly over
Their far-off clamour from overhead.
They are flying west, by their instinct guided,
And for man likewise is his fate decided,
And griefs apportioned and joys divided
By a mighty power with a purpose dread.

The All Right 'Un

He came from 'further out',
That land of heat and drought
And dust and gravel.
He got a touch of sun,
And rested at the run
Until his cure was done,
And he could travel.

When spring had decked the plain,
He flitted off again
As flit the swallows.
And from that western land,
When many months were spanned,
A letter came to hand,
Which read as follows:

'Dear sir, I take my pen
In hopes that all your men
And you are hearty.
You think that I've forgot
Your kindness, Mr Scott,
Oh, no, dear sir, I'm not
That sort of party.

'You sometimes bet, I know,
Well, now you'll have a show
The 'books' to frighten.
Up here at Wingadee
Young Billy Fife and me
We're training Strife, and he
Is a all right 'un.

'Just now we're running byes,
But, sir, first time he tries
I'll send you word of.
And running 'on the crook'
Their measures we have took,
It is the deadest hook
You ever heard of.

'So when we lets him go,
Why, then, I'll let you know
And you can have a show
To put a mite on.
Now, sir, my leave I'll take,
Yours truly, William Blake.
P.S.—Make no mistake,
He's a all right 'un.'

By next week's *Riverine*
I saw my friend had been
A bit too cunning.
I read: 'The racehorse Strife
And jockey William Fife
Disqualified for life—
Suspicious running.'

But though they spoilt his game,
I reckon all the same

I fairly ought to claim
My friend a white 'un.
For though he wasn't straight,
His deeds would indicate
His heart at any rate
Was 'a all right 'un'.

The Great Calamity

MacFierce'un came to Whiskeyhurst
When summer days were hot,
And bided there wi' Jock McThirst,
A brawny brother Scot.
Gude Faith! They made the whisky fly,
Like Highland chieftains true,
And when they'd drunk the beaker dry
They sang 'We are nae fou!'

'There is nae folk like oor ain folk,
Sae gallant and sae true.'
They sang the only Scottish joke
Which is, 'We are nae fou.'

Said bold McThirst, 'Let Saxons jaw
Aboot their great concerns,
But bonny Scotland beats them a',
The land o' cakes and Burns,
The land o' partridge, deer, and grouse,
Fill up your glass, I beg,
There's muckle whusky i' the house,
Forbye what's in the keg.'

And here a hearty laugh he laughed,
Just come wi' me, I beg.'
MacFierce'un saw with pleasure daft
A fifty-gallon keg.

'Losh, man, that's grand,' MacFierce'un cried,
Saw ever man the like,
Noo, wi' the daylight, I maun ride
To meet a Southron tyke,
But I'll be back ere summer's gone,
So bide for me, I beg,
We'll make a grand assault upon
Yon deevil of a keg.'

* * *

MacFierce'un rode to Whiskeyhurst,
When summer days were gone,
And there he met with Jock McThirst
Was greetin' all alone.
'McThirst what gars ye look sae blank?
Have all yer wits gane daft?
Has that accursed Southron bank
Called up your overdraft?
Is all your grass burnt up wi' drouth?
Is wool and hides gone flat?'
McThirst replied, 'Gude friend, in truth,
'Tis muckle waur than that.'

'Has sair misfortune cursed your life
That you should weep sae free?
Is harm upon your bonny wife,
The children at your knee?
Is scaith upon your house and hame?'
McThirst upraised his head:
'My bairns hae done the deed of shame—
'Twere better they were dead.
To think my bonny infant son
Should do the deed o' guilt—
He let the whuskey spigot run,
And a' the whuskey's spilt?'

* * *

Upon them both these words did bring
A solemn silence deep,
Gude faith, it is a fearsome thing
To see two strong men weep.

A Bush Christening

On the outer Barcoo where the churches are few
And men of religion are scanty,
On a road never cross'd 'cept by folk that are lost,
One Michael Magee had a shanty.

Now this Mike was the dad of a ten year old lad,
Plump, healthy, and stoutly conditioned;
He was strong as the best, but poor Mike had no rest
For the youngster had never been christened.

And his wife used to cry, 'If the darlin' should die
Saint Peter would not recognise him.'
But by luck he survived till a preacher arrived,
Who agreed straightaway to baptise him.

Now the artful young rogue, while they held their collogue,
With his ear to the keyhole was listenin',
And he muttered in fright, while his features turned white,
'What the divil and all is this christenin'?'

He was none of your dolts, he had seen them brand colts,
And it seemed to his small understanding,
If the man in the frock made him one of the flock,
It must mean something very like branding.

So away with a rush he set off for the bush,
While the tears in his eyelids they glistened—
''Tis outrageous,' says he, 'to brand youngsters like me,
I'll be dashed if I'll stop to be christened !'

Like a young native dog he ran into a log,
And his father with language uncivil,
Never heeding the 'praste' cried aloud in his haste,
'Come out and be christened, you divil !'

But he lay there as snug as a bug in a rug,
And his parents in vain might reprove him,
Till his reverence spoke (he was fond of a joke)
I've a notion,' says he, 'that'll move him.

'Poke a stick up the log, give the spalpeen a prog;
Poke him aisy—don't hurt him or maim him,
'Tis not long that he'll stand, I've the water at hand,
As he rushes out this end I'll name him.

'Here he comes, and for shame! ye've forgotten the name—
Is it Patsy or Michael or Dinnis?'
Here the youngster ran out, and the priest gave a shout—
'Take your chance, anyhow, wid "Maginnis"!'

As the howling young cub ran away to the scrub
Where he knew that pursuit would be risky,
The priest, as he fled, flung a flask at his head
That was labelled *Maginnis's Whisky!*

And Maginnis Magee has been made a J.P.,
And the one thing he hates more than sin is
To be asked by the folk, who have heard of the joke,
How he came to be christened 'Maginnis'!

Frying Pan's Theology

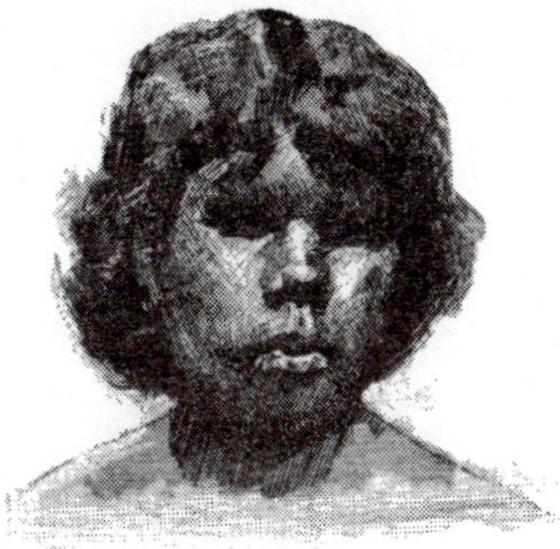

Scene: On Monaro.
Dramatis Personae:
Shock-headed blackfellow,
Boy (on a pony).
Snowflakes are falling
So gentle and slow,
Youngster says, 'Frying Pan,
What makes it snow?'
Frying Pan confident
Makes the reply—
'Shake 'im big flour bag
Up in the sky!'

'What! when there's miles of it!
Sur'ly that's brag.
Who is there strong enough
Shake such a bag?'
'What parson tellin' you,
Ole Mister Dodd,
Tell you in Sunday-school?
Big feller God!
He drive 'im bullock dray,
Then thunder go,
He shake 'im flour bag—
Tumble down snow!'

Last Week

Oh, the new-chum went to the back block run,
But he should have gone there last week.
He tramped ten miles with a loaded gun,
But of turkey or duck he saw never a one,
For he should have been there last week,
They said,
There were flocks of 'em there last week.

He wended his way to a waterfall,
And he should have gone there last week.
He carried a camera, legs and all,
But the day was hot, and the stream was small,
For he should have gone there last week,
They said,
They drowned a man there last week.

He went for a drive, and he made a start,
Which should have been made last week,
For the old horse died of a broken heart;
So he footed it home and he dragged the cart—
But the horse was all right last week,
They said,
He trotted a match last week.

So he asked the bushies who came from far
To visit the town last week,
If they'd dine with him, and they said 'Hurrah'!
But there wasn't a drop in the whisky jar—
You should have been here last week,
He said,
I drank it all up last week!

The Ghost of the Murderer's Hut

My horse had been lamed in the foot
In the rocks at the back of the run,
So I camped at the Murderer's Hut,
At the place where the murder was done.

The walls were all spattered with gore,
A terrible symbol of guilt;
And the bloodstains were fresh on the floor
Where the blood of the victim was spilt.

The wind hurried past with a shout,
The thunderstorm doubled its din
As I shrank from the danger without,
And recoiled from the horror within.

When lo! at the window a shape,
A creature of infinite dread;
A thing with the face of an ape,
And with eyes like the eyes of the dead.

With the horns of a fiend, and a skin
That was hairy as satyr or elf,
And a long, pointed beard on its chin—
My God! 'twas the Devil himself.

In anguish I sank on the floor,
With terror my features were stiff,
Till *the thing* gave a kind of a roar,
Ending up with a resonant 'Biff!'

Then a cheer burst aloud from my throat,
For the thing that my spirit did vex
Was naught but an elderly goat—
Just a goat of the masculine sex.

When his master was killed he had fled,
And now, by the dingoes bereft,
The nannies were all of them dead,
And only the billy was left.

So we had him brought in on a stage
To the house where, in style, he can strut,
And he lives to a fragrant old age
As the Ghost of the Murderer's Hut.

Shearing at Castlereagh

The bell is set a-ringing, and the engine gives a toot,
There's five and thirty shearers here a-shearing for the loot,
So stir yourselves, you penners-up and shove the sheep along,
The musterers are fetching them a hundred thousand strong,
And make your collie dogs speak up—what would the buyers say
In London if the wool was late this year from Castlereagh?

The man that 'rung' the Tubbo shed is not the ringer here,
That stripling from the Cooma side can teach him how to shear.
They trim away the ragged locks, and rip the cutter goes,
And leaves a track of snowy fleece from brisket to the nose;

It's lovely how they peel it off with never stop nor stay,
They're racing for the ringer's place this year at Castlereagh.

The man that keeps the cutters sharp is growling in his cage,
He's always in a hurry and he's always in a rage—
"You clumsy-fisted muttonheads, you'd turn a fellow sick,
You pass yourselves as shearers? You were born to swing a pick!
Another broken cutter here, that's two you've broke today,
It's awful how such crawlers come to shear at Castlereagh.'

The youngsters picking up the fleece enjoy the merry din,
They throw the classer up the fleece, he throws it to the bin;
The pressers standing by the rack are waiting for the wool,
There's room for just a couple more, the press is nearly full;
Now jump upon the lever, lads, and heave and heave away,
Another bale of golden fleece is branded 'Castlereagh'.

The Travelling Post Office

The roving breezes come and go, the reed beds sweep and sway,
The sleepy river murmurs low, and loiters on its way,
It is the land of lots o' time along the Castlereagh.

* * *

The old man's son had left the farm, he found it dull and slow,
He drifted to the great North-west where all the rovers go.
'He's gone so long,' the old man said, 'he's dropped right out of mind,
But if you'd write a line to him I'd take it very kind;
He's shearing here and fencing there, a kind of waif and stray,
He's droving now with Conroy's sheep along the Castlereagh.
The sheep are travelling for the grass, and travelling very slow;
They may be at Mundooran now, or past the Overflow,
Or tramping down the black soil flats across by Waddiwong,
But all those little country towns would send the letter wrong,
The mailman, if he's extra tired, would pass them in his sleep,
It's safest to address the note to "Care of Conroy's sheep".
For five and twenty thousand head can scarcely go astray,
You write to "Care of Conroy's sheep along the Castlereagh".'

* * *

By rock and ridge and riverside the western mail has gone,

Across the great Blue Mountain Range to take that letter on.
A moment on the topmost grade while open fire doors glare,
She pauses like a living thing to breathe the mountain air,
Then launches down the other side across the plains away
To bear that note to 'Conroy's sheep along the Castlereagh'.

And now by coach and mailman's bag it goes from town to town,
And Conroy's Gap and Conroy's Creek have marked it 'further down'.
Beneath a sky of deepest blue where never cloud abides,
A speck upon the waste of plain the lonely mailman rides.
Where fierce hot winds have set the pine and myall boughs asweep
He hails the shearers passing by for news of Conroy's sheep.
By big lagoons where wildfowl play and crested pigeons flock,
By campfires where the drovers ride around their restless stock,
And pass the teamster toiling down to fetch the wool away
My letter chases Conroy's sheep along the Castlereagh.

A Bunch of Roses

Roses ruddy and roses white,
What are the joys that my heart discloses?
Sitting alone in the fading light
Memories come to me here to-night
With the wonderful scent of the big red roses.

Memories come as the daylight fades
Down on the hearth where the firelight dozes;
Flicker and flutter the lights and shades,
And I see the face of a queen of maids
Whose memory comes with the scent of roses.

Visions arise of a scene of mirth,
And a ballroom belle that superbly poses—
A queenly woman of queenly worth,
And I am the happiest man on earth
With a single flower from a bunch of roses.

Only her memory lives tonight—
God in His wisdom her young life closes;
Over her grave may the turf be light,
Cover her coffin with roses white—
She was always fond of the big white roses.

* * *

Such are visions that fade away—
Man proposes and God disposes;
Look in the glass and I see to-day
Only an old man, worn and grey,
Bending his head to a bunch of roses.

Ambition and Art

Ambition

I am the maid of the lustrous eyes
Of great fruition,
Whom the sons of men that are over-wise
Have called Ambition.

And the world's success is the only goal
I have within me;
The meanest man with the smallest soul
May woo and win me.

For the lust of power and the pride of place
To all I proffer.
Wilt thou take thy part in the crowded race
For what I offer?

The choice is thine, and the world is wide—
Thy path is lonely.
I may not lead and I may not guide—
I urge thee only.

I am just a whip and a spur that smites
To fierce endeavour.
In the restless days and the sleepless nights
I urge thee ever.

Thou shalt wake from sleep with a startled cry,
In fright upleaping
At a rival's step as it passes by
Whilst thou art sleeping.

Honour and truth shall be overthrown
In fierce desire;
Thou shalt use thy friend as a stepping-stone
To mount thee higher.

When the curtain falls on the sordid strife
That seemed so splendid,
Thou shalt look with pain on the wasted life
That thou hast ended.

Thou hast sold thy life for a guerdon small
In fitful flashes;
There has been reward—but the end of all
Is dust and ashes.

For the night has come and it brings to naught
Thy projects cherished,
And thine epitaph shall in brass be wrought—
'He lived, and perished.'

Art

I wait for thee at the outer gate,
My love, mine only;
Wherefore tarriest thou so late
While I am lonely.

Thou shalt seek my side with a footstep swift,
In thee implanted
Is the love of Art and the greatest gift
That God has granted.

And the world's concerns with its rights and wrongs
Shall seem but small things—
Poet or painter, a singer of songs,
Thine art is all things.

For the wine of life is a woman's love
To keep beside thee;
But the love of Art is a thing above—
A star to guide thee.

As the years go by with thy love of Art
All undiminished,
Thou shalt end thy days with a quiet heart—
Thy work is finished.

So the painter fashions a picture strong
That fadeth never,
And the singer singeth a wond'rous song
That lives for ever.

How Gilbert Died

There's never a stone at the sleeper's head,
There's never a fence beside,
And the wandering stock on the grave may tread
Unnoticed and undenied,
But the smallest child on the Watershed
Can tell you how Gilbert died.

For he rode at dusk, with his comrade Dunn
To the hut at the Stockman's Ford,
In the waning light of the sinking sun
They peered with a fierce accord.
They were outlaws both—and on each man's head
Was a thousand pounds reward.

They had taken toll of the country round,
And the troopers came behind
With a black that tracked like a human hound
In the scrub and the ranges blind:
He could run the trail where a white man's eye
No sign of a track could find.

He had hunted them out of the One Tree Hill
And over the Old Man Plain,
But they wheeled their tracks with a wild beast's skill,
And they made for the range again.
Then away to the hut where their grandsire dwelt,
They rode with a loosened rein.

And their grandsire gave them a greeting bold:
'Come in and rest in peace,
No safer place does the country hold—
With the night pursuit must cease,
And we'll drink success to the roving boys,
And to hell with the black police.'

But they went to death when they entered there,
In the hut at the Stockman's Ford,
For their grandsire's words were as false as fair—
They were doomed to the hangman's cord.
He had sold them both to the black police
For the sake of the big reward.

In the depth of night there are forms that glide
As stealthy as serpents creep,
And around the hut where the outlaws hide
They plant in the shadows deep,
And they wait till the first faint flush of dawn
Shall waken their prey from sleep.

But Gilbert wakes while the night is dark—
A restless sleeper, aye,
He has heard the sound of a sheep-dog's bark,
And his horse's warning neigh,
And he says to his mate, 'There are hawks abroad,
And it's time that we went away.'

Their rifles stood at the stretcher head,
Their bridles lay to hand,
They wakened the old man out of his bed,
When they heard the sharp command:
'In the name of the Queen lay down your arms,
Now, Dunn and Gilbert, stand!'

Then Gilbert reached for his rifle true
That close at his hand he kept,
He pointed it straight at the voice and drew,
But never a flash outleapt,
For the water ran from the rifle breech—
It was drenched while the outlaws slept.

Then he dropped the piece with a bitter oath,
And he turned to his comrade Dunn:
'We are sold,' he said, 'we are dead men both,
But there may be a chance for one;
I'll stop and I'll fight with the pistol here,
You take to your heels and run.'

So Dunn crept out on his hands and knees
In the dim, half-dawning light,
And he made his way to a patch of trees,
And vanished among the night,
And the trackers hunted his tracks all day,
But they never could trace his flight.

But Gilbert walked from the open door
In a confident style and rash;
He heard at his side the rifles roar,
And he heard the bullets crash.
But he laughed as he lifted his pistol-hand,
And he fired at the rifle flash.

Then out of the shadows the troopers aimed
At his voice and the pistol sound,
With the rifle flashes the darkness flamed,
He staggered and spun around,
And they riddled his body with rifle balls
As it lay on the blood-soaked ground.

There's never a stone at the sleeper's head,
There's never a fence beside,
And the wandering stock on the grave may tread
Unnoticed and undenied,
But the smallest child on the Watershed
Can tell you how Gilbert died.

A Voice from the Town

I thought, in the days of the droving,
Of steps I might hope to retrace,
To be done with the bush and the roving
And settle once more in my place.
With a heart that was well nigh to breaking,
In the long, lonely rides on the plain,
I thought of the pleasure of taking
The hand of a lady again.

I am back into civilisation,
Once more in the stir and the strife,
But the old joys have lost their sensation—
The light has gone out of my life;
The men of my time they have married,
Made fortunes or gone to the wall;
Too long from the scene I have tarried,
And, somehow, I'm out of it all.

For I go to the balls and the races
A lonely companionless elf,
And the ladies bestow all their graces
On others less grey than myself;
While the talk goes around I'm a dumb one
'Midst youngsters that chatter and prate,
And they call me 'the Man who was Someone
Way back in the year Sixty-eight'.
And I look, sour and old, at the dancers
That swing to the strains of the band,
And the ladies all give me the Lancers,
No waltzes—I quite understand.
For matrons intent upon matching
Their daughters with infinite push,
Would scarce think him worthy the catching,
The broken-down man from the bush.

New partners have come and new faces,
And I, of the bygone brigade,
Sharply feel that oblivion my place is
I must lie with the rest in the shade.
And the youngsters, fresh-featured and pleasant,
They live as we lived—fairly fast;
But I doubt if the men of the present
Are as good as the men of the past.

Of excitement and praise they are chary,
There is nothing much good upon earth;
Their watchword is *nil admirari,*
They are bored from the days of their birth.
Where the life that we led was a revel
They 'wince and relent and refrain'—
I could show them the road—to the devil,
Were I only a youngster again.

I could show them the road where the stumps are
The pleasures that end in remorse,
And the game where the Devil's three trumps are,
The woman, the card, and the horse.
Shall the blind lead the blind—shall the sower
Of wind reap the storm as of yore?
Though they get to their goal somewhat slower,
They march where we hurried before.

For the world never learns—just as we did,
They gallantly go to their fate,
Unheeded all warnings, unheeded
The maxims of elders sedate.
As the husbandman, patiently toiling,
Draws a harvest each year from the soil,
So the fools grow afresh for the spoiling,
And a new crop of thieves for the spoil.

But a truce to this dull moralising,
  Let them drink while the drops are of gold,
I have tasted the dregs—'twere surprising
  Were the new wine to me like the old;

And I weary for lack of employment
  In idleness day after day,
For the key to the door of enjoyment
  Is Youth—and I've thrown it away.

Tommy Corrigan

You talk of riders on the flat, of nerve and pluck and pace—
Not one in fifty has the nerve to ride a steeplechase.
It's right enough, while horses pull and take their fences strong,
To rush a flier to the front and bring the field along;
But what about the last half-mile, with horses blown and beat—
When every jump means all you know to keep him on his feet?

When any slip means sudden death—with wife and child to keep—
It needs some nerve to draw the whip and flog him at the leap—
But Corrigan would ride them out, by danger undismayed,
He never flinched at fence or wall, he never was afraid;
With easy seat and nerve of steel, light hand and smiling face,
He held the rushing horses back, and made the sluggards race.

He gave the shirkers extra heart, he steadied down the rash,
He rode great clumsy boring brutes, and chanced a fatal smash;
He got the rushing Wymlet home that never jumped at all—
But clambered over every fence and clouted every wall.
You should have heard the cheers, my boys, that shook the members' stand
Whenever Tommy Corrigan weighed out to ride Lone Hand.

They were, indeed, a glorious pair—the great upstanding horse,
The gamest jockey on his back that ever faced a course.
Though weight was big and pace was hot and fences stiff and tall,
'You follow Tommy Corrigan' was passed to one and all.
And every man on Ballarat raised all he could command
To put on Tommy Corrigan when riding old Lone Hand.

But now we'll keep his memory green while horsemen come and go;
We may not see his like again where silks and satins glow.
We'll drink to him in silence, boys—he's followed down the track
Where many a good man went before, but never one came back.
And, let us hope, in that far land where the shades of brave men reign,
The gallant Tommy Corrigan will ride Lone Hand again.

How the Favourite Beat Us

'Aye,' said the boozer, 'I tell you it's true, sir,
I once was a punter with plenty of pelf,
But gone is my glory, I'll tell you the story
How I stiffened my horse and got stiffened myself.

' 'Twas a mare called the Cracker, I came down to back her,
But found she was favourite all of a rush,
The folk just did pour on to lay six to four on,
And several bookies were killed in the crush.

'It seems old Tomato was stiff, though a starter;
They reckoned him fit for the Caulfield to keep.
The Bloke and the Donah were scratched by their owner,
He only was offered three-fourths of the sweep.

'We knew Salamander was slow as a gander,
The mare could have beat him the length of the straight,
And old Manumission was out of condition,
And most of the others were running off weight.

'No doubt someone "blew it", for everyone knew it
The bets were all gone, and I muttered in spite,
"If I can't get a copper, by Jingo, I'll stop her,
Let the public fall in, it will serve the brutes right."

'I said to the jockey, "Now, listen, my cocky,
You watch as you're cantering down by the stand,
I'll wait where that toff is and give you the office,
You're only to win if I lift up my hand."

'I then tried to back her—"What price is the Cracker?"
"Our books are all full, sir" each bookie did swear;
My mind, then, I made up, my fortune I played up
I bet every shilling against my own mare.

'I strolled to the gateway, the mare in the straight way
Was shifting and dancing, and pawing the ground,
The boy saw me enter and wheeled for his canter,
When a darned great mosquito came buzzing around.

'They breed 'em at Hexham, it's risky to vex 'em
They suck a man dry at a sitting, no doubt,
But just as the mare passed, he fluttered my hair past,
I lifted my hand, and I flattened him out.

'I was stunned when they started, the mare simply darted
Away to the front when the flag was let fall,
For none there could match her, and none tried to catch her—
She finished a furlong in front of them all.

'You bet that I went for the boy, whom I sent for
The moment he weighed and came out of the stand—
"Who paid you to win it? Come, own up this minute."
"Lord love yer," said he, "why, you lifted your hand."

' 'Twas true, by St Peter, that cursed "musketeer"
Had broke me so broke that I hadn't a brown,
And you'll find the best course is when dealing with horses
To win when you're able, and *keep your hands down.*'

The Amateur Rider

Him going to ride for us! *Him*—with the pants and the eyeglass and all
Amateur! don't he just look it—it's twenty to one on a fall.
Boss must be gone off his head to be sending our steeplechase crack
Out over fences like these with an object like that on his back.

Ride! Don't tell *me* he can ride. With his pants just as loose as balloons,
How can he sit on his horse? and his spurs like a pair of harpoons;
Ought to be under the Dog Act, he ought, and be kept off the course.
Fall! why, he'd fall off a cart, let alone off a steeplechase horse.

* * *

Yessir! the 'orse is all ready—I wish you'd have rode him before;
Nothing like knowing your 'orse, sir, and this chap's a terror to bore;
Battleaxe always could pull, and he rushes his fences like fun—
Stands off his jump twenty feet, and then springs like a shot from a gun.

Oh, he can jump 'em all right, sir, you make no mistake, 'e's a toff;
Clouts 'em in earnest, too, sometimes, you mind that he don't clout you off—
Don't seem to mind how he hits 'em, his shins is as hard as a nail,
Sometimes you'll see the fence shake and the splinters fly up from the rail.

All you can do is to hold him and just let him jump as he likes,
Give him his head at the fences, and hang on like death if he strikes;
Don't let him run himself out—you can lie third or fourth in the race—
Until you clear the stone wall, and from that you can put on the pace.

Fell at that wall once, he did, and it gave him a regular spread,
Ever since that time he flies it—he'll stop if you pull at his head,
Just let him race—you can trust him—he'll take first-class care he don't fall,
And I think that's the lot—but remember, *he must have his head at the wall.*

* * *

Well, he's down safe as far as the start, and he seems to sit on pretty neat,
Only his baggified breeches would ruinate anyone's seat—
They're away—here they come—the first fence, and he's head over heels for a crown!
Good for the new chum, he's over, and two of the others are down!

Now for the treble, my hearty—By Jove, he can ride, after all;
Whoop, that's your sort—let him fly them! He hasn't much fear of a fall.
Who in the world would have thought it? And aren't they just going a pace?
Little Recruit in the lead there will make it a stoutly-run race.
Lord! But they're racing in earnest—and down goes Recruit on his head,

Rolling clean over his boy—it's a miracle if he ain't dead.
Battleaxe, Battleaxe, yet! By the Lord, he's got most of 'em beat—
Ho! did you see how he struck, and the swell never moved in his seat?

Second time round, and, by Jingo! he's holding his lead of 'em well;
Hark to him clouting the timber! It don't seem to trouble the swell.
Now for the wall—let him rush it. A thirty-foot leap, I declare—
Never a shift in his seat, and he's racing for home like a hare.

What's that that's chasing him—Rataplan—regular demon to stay!
Sit down and ride for your life now! Oh, good, that's the style—come away
Rataplan's certain to beat you, unless you can give him the slip;
Sit down and rub in the whalebone now—give him the spurs and the whip!

Battleaxe, Battleaxe, yet—and it's Battleaxe wins for a crown;
Look at him rushing the fences, he wants to bring t'other chap down.
Rataplan never will catch him if only he keeps on his pins;
Now! the last fence! and he's over it! Battleaxe, Battleaxe wins!

* * *

Well, sir, you rode him just perfect—I knew from the first you could ride.
Some of the chaps said you couldn't, an' I says just like this a' one side:
Mark me, I says, that's a tradesman—the saddle is where he was bred.
Weight! you're all right, sir, and thank you; and them was the words that I said.

The Man Who Was Away

The widow sought the lawyer's room with children three in tow,
She told the lawyer man her tale in tones of deepest woe.
Said she, 'My husband took to drink for pains in his inside,
And never drew a sober breath from then until he died.

'He never drew a sober breath, he died without a will,
And I must sell the bit of land the childer's mouths to fill.
There's some is grown and gone away, but some is childer yet,
And times is very bad indeed—a livin's hard to get.

'There's Min and Sis and little Chris, they stops at home with me,
And Sal has married Greenhide Bill that breaks for Bingeree.

And Fred is drovin' Conroy's sheep along the Castlereagh,
And Charley's shearin' down the Bland, and Peter is away.'

The lawyer wrote the details down in ink of legal blue—
'There's Minnie, Susan, Christopher, they stop at home with you;
There's Sarah, Frederick, and Charles, I'll write to them to-day,
But what about the other one—the one who is away?

'You'll have to furnish his consent to sell the bit of land.'
The widow shuffled in her seat, 'Oh, don't you understand?
I thought a lawyer ought to know—I don't know what to say—
You'll have to do without him, boss, for Peter is away.'

But here the little boy spoke up—said he, 'We thought you knew;
He's done six months in Goulburn gaol—he's got six more to do.'
Thus in one comprehensive flash he made it clear as day,
The mystery of Peter's life—the man who was away.

Saltbush Bill

Now this is the law of the Overland that all in the West obey,
A man must cover with travelling sheep a six-mile stage a day;
But this is the law which the drovers make, right easily understood,
They travel their stage where the grass is bad, but they camp where the grass is good;
They camp, and they ravage the squatter's grass till never a blade remains,
Then they drift away as the white clouds drift on the edge of the saltbush plains,
From camp to camp and from run to run they battle it hand to hand,
For a blade of grass and the right to pass on the track of the Overland.

For this is the law of the Great Stock Routes, 'tis written in white and black—
The man that goes with a travelling mob must keep to a half-mile track;
And the drovers keep to a half-mile track on the runs where the grass is dead,

But they spread their sheep on a well-grassed run till they go with a two-mile spread.
So the squatters hurry the drovers on from dawn till the fall of night,
And the squatters' dogs and the drovers' dogs get mixed in a deadly fight;
Yet the squatters' men, though they hunt the mob, are willing the peace to keep,
For the drovers learn how to use their hands when they go with the travelling sheep;
But this is the tale of a Jackaroo that came from a foreign strand,
And the fight that he fought with Saltbush Bill, the King of the Overland.

Now Saltbush Bill was a drover tough, as ever the country knew,
He had fought his way on the Great Stock Routes from the sea to the Big Barcoo;
He could tell when he came to a friendly run that gave him a chance to spread,
And he knew where the hungry owners were that hurried his sheep ahead;
He was drifting down in the Eighty drought with a mob that could scarcely creep,
(When the kangaroos by the thousands starve, it is rough on the travelling sheep.)
And he camped one night at the crossing place on the edge of the Wilga run,
'We must manage a feed for them here,' he said, 'or the half of the mob are done!'
So he spread them out when they left the camp wherever they liked to go,
Till he grew aware of a Jackaroo with a station hand in tow,
And they set to work on the straggling sheep, and with many a stockwhip crack
They forced them in where the grass was dead in the space of the half-mile track;

So William prayed that the hand of fate might suddenly strike him blue
But he'd get some grass for his starving sheep in the teeth of that Jackaroo.
So he turned and he cursed the Jackaroo, he cursed him alive or dead,
From the soles of his great unwieldy feet to the crown of his ugly head,
With an extra curse on the moke he rode and the cur at his heels that ran,
Till the Jackaroo from his horse got down and he went for the drover man;
With the station hand for his picker-up, though the sheep ran loose the while,
They battled it out on the saltbush plain in the regular prize ring style.

Now, the new chum fought for his honour's sake and the pride of the English race,
But the drover fought for his daily bread with a smile on his bearded face;
So he shifted ground and he sparred for wind and he made it a lengthy mill,
And from time to time as his scouts came in they whispered to Saltbush Bill—
"We have spread the sheep with a two-mile spread, and the grass it is something grand,
You must stick to him, Bill, for another round for the pride of the Overland.'

The new chum made it a rushing fight, though never a blow got home,
Till the sun rode in the cloudless sky and glared on the brick-red loam,
Till the sheep drew in to the shelter trees and settled them down to rest,
Then the drover said he would fight no more and he gave his opponent best.

So the new chum rode to the homestead straight and he told them a story grand
Of the desperate fight that he fought that day with the King of the Overland.
And the tale went home to the public schools of the pluck of the English swell,
How the drover fought for his very life, but blood in the end must tell.

But the travelling sheep and the Wilga sheep were boxed on the Old Man Plain.
'Twas a full week's work ere they drafted out and hunted them off again,
With a week's good grass in their wretched hides, with a curse and a stockwhip crack,
They hunted them off on the road once more to starve on the half-mile track.
And Saltbush Bill, on the Overland, will many a time recite
How the best day's work that ever he did was the day that he lost the fight.

The Two Devines

It was shearing-time at the Myall Lake,
And there rose the sound thro' the livelong day
Of the constant clash that the shear-blades make
When the fastest shearers are making play,
But there wasn't a man in the shearers' lines
That could shear a sheep with the two Devines.

They had rung the sheds of the east and west,
Had beaten the cracks of the Walgett side,
And the Cooma shearers had giv'n them best—
When they saw them shear, they were satisfied.
From the southern slopes to the western pines
They were noted men, were the two Devines.

'Twas a wether flock that had come to hand,
Great struggling brutes, that the shearers shirk,
For the fleece was filled with the grass and sand,
And seventy sheep was a big day's work.
'At a pound a hundred it's dashed hard lines
To shear such sheep,' said the two Devines.

But the shearers knew that they'd make a cheque
When they came to deal with the station ewes;
They were bare of belly and bare of neck
With a fleece as light as a kangaroo's.
'We will show the boss how a shear-blade shines
When we reach those ewes,' said the two Devines.

But it chanced next day when the stunted pines
Were swayed and stirred with the dawn-wind's breath,
That a message came for the two Devines
That their father lay at the point of death.
So away at speed through the whispering pines
Down the bridle track rode the two Devines.

It was fifty miles to their father's hut,
And the dawn was bright when they rode away;
At the fall of night when the shed was shut
And the men had rest from the toilsome day,
To the shed once more through the dark'ning pines
On their weary steeds came the two Devines.

'Well, you're back right sudden,' the super. said;
'Is the old man dead and the funeral done?'
'Well, no, sir, he ain't not exactly dead,
But as good as dead,' said the eldest son—
'And we couldn't bear such a chance to lose,
So we came straight back to tackle the ewes.'

* * *

They are shearing ewes at the Myall Lake,
And the shed is merry the livelong day
With the clashing sound that the shear-blades make
When the fastest shearers are making play,
And a couple of 'hundred and ninety-nines'
Are the tallies made by the two Devines.

Castlebar

Bidding good morrow to all our cares,
Riding along with a joyful heart,
Little we reck of the world's affairs,
All that we ask is a decent start.
Though the jumps are big and the distance far
We will get to the finish on Castlebar.

Little Blue Peter goes sailing by;
Little Blue Peter may stand or fall
For his rider reckons no man can die
Till his day comes round—so he chances all!
And away to the front where the good ones are
Go Little Blue Peter and Castlebar.

Bay and chestnut and brown and black,
I hear in the timber their hoof beats drum,
As I clear the fence on the Prospect track
I turn in the saddle and watch them come.
But the chestnut horse with the big white star.
Why isn't he following Castlebar?

Dear little woman with eyes of blue,
With lissom figure and easy grace,
I turn in the saddle and long for you
As the field sweeps on at a rattling pace.
But I know that away on the heights afar
Your heart is following Castlebar.

Here's Luck

A TOAST AT A HUNT CLUB DINNER

It chanced one day I watched a steeplechase,
And one horse singled out and led them all
Across the fences at a rattling pace
Until he hit a fence and took a fall.
His rider laughed and muttered with a smile—
'Well, anyhow, I led 'em for a while.'

And this the text is for my theme tonight—
A moral that the wisest men have sung:
Our life is very short—and swift the flight
Of time—so, comrades, go it while young.
And when old age comes on you'll find it good
To think you made the running while you could.

There's nothing now too solid or too high
For some of you to take and chance a spill;
But we must funk the fences bye and bye,
When limbs grow stiff and hands have lost their skill.
In wintry age we'll seek the hearthstone's blaze;
So let us make the most of youth's bright days.

So now, my friends, good luck and may you keep
Stout hearts and true and honest kindly mirth,
When drawing nearer to the last great leap
That lands us on the other side of earth,
Where many a gallant horseman and brave steed
Has gone before to give us all a lead.

Waltzing Matilda

Once a jolly swagman camped by a billabong,
    Under the shade of a coolibah tree,
And he sang as he watched and waited 'til his billy boiled,
    'Who'll come a-waltzing Matilda with me—
Waltzing Matilda, waltzing Matilda, who'll come a-waltzing
    Matilda with me?'
And he sang as he watched and waited 'til his billy boiled,
    'Who'll come a-waltzing Matilda with me?'

Down came a jumbuck to drink at the billabong
    Up jumped the swagman and grabbed him with glee,
And he sang, as he stowed that jumbuck in his tucker-bag,
    'Who'll come a-waltzing Matilda with me?
Waltzing Matilda, waltzing Matilda, who'll come a-waltzing
    Matilda with me?'
And he sang as he stowed that jumbuck in his tucker-bag,
    'Who'll come a-waltzing Matilda with me?'

Up came the squatter, mounted on his thoroughbred,
    Down came the troopers—one, two, three—
'Whose is the jolly jumbuck, you've got in your tucker-bag?
    You'll come a-waltzing Matilda with me.
Waltzing Matilda, waltzing Matilda, who'll come a-waltzing
    Matilda with me?
Whose is the jolly jumbuck you've got in your tucker-bag.
    You'll come a-waltzing Matilda with me.'

Up jumped the swagman, and sprang into the billabong,
    'You'll never take me alive!' said he.
And his ghost may be heard, as we pass by that billabong,
    'Who'll come a-waltzing Matilda with me?
Waltzing Matilda, waltzing Matilda,
    Who'll come a-waltzing Matilda with me?'
And his ghost may be heard, as we pass by that billabong,
    'Who'll come a-waltzing Matilda with me?'

Johnson's Antidote

Down along the Snakebite River, where the overlanders camp,
Where the serpents are in millions, all of the most deadly stamp;
Where the station-cook in terror, nearly every time he bakes,
Mixes up among the doughboys half-a-dozen poison-snakes:
Where the wily free-selector walks in armour-plated pants,
And defies the stings of scorpions, and the bites of bull-dog ants:
Where the adder and the viper tear each other by the throat,
There it was that William Johnson sought his snakebite antidote.
Johnson was a free-selector, and his brain went rather queer,
For the constant sight of serpents filled him with a deadly fear;
So he tramped his free-selection, morning, afternoon, and night,
Seeking for some great specific that would cure the serpent's bite.
Till King Billy, of the Mooki, chieftain of the flourbag head,
Told him, 'Spos'n snake bite pfeller, pfeller mostly drop down dead;
Spos'n snake bite old goanna, then you watch a while you see,
Old goanna cure himself with eating little pfeller tree.'
'That's the cure,' said William Johnson, 'point me out this plant sublime,'
But King Billy, feeling lazy, said he'd go another time.
Thus it came to pass that Johnson, having got the tale by rote,
Followed every stray goanna, seeking for the antidote.

Loafing once beside the river, while he thought his heart would break,
There he saw a big goanna fighting with a tiger snake,
In and out they rolled and wriggled, bit each other, heart and soul,
Till the valiant old goanna swallowed his opponent whole.
Breathless, Johnson sat and watched him, saw him struggle up the bank,
Saw him nibbling at the branches of some bushes, green and rank;
Saw him, happy and contented, lick his lips, as off he crept,
While the bulging in his stomach showed where his opponent slept.
Then a cheer of exultation burst aloud from Johnson's throat;
'Luck at last,' said he, 'I've struck it! 'tis the famous antidote.

'Here it is, the Grand Elixir, greatest blessing ever known,
Twenty thousand men in India die each year of snakes alone.
Think of all the foreign nations, negro, chow, and blackamoor,
Saved from sudden expiration, by my wondrous snakebite cure.
It will bring me fame and fortune! In the happy days to be,
Men of every clime and nation will be round to gaze on me—
'Scientific men in thousands, men of mark and men of note,
Rushing down the Mooki River, after Johnson's antidote.
It will cure *delirium tremens,* when the patient's eyeballs stare
At imaginary spiders, snakes which really are not there.

When he thinks he sees them wriggle, when he thinks he sees them bloat,
It will cure him just to think of Johnson's Snakebite Antidote.'

Then he rushed to the museum, found a scientific man—
'Trot me out a deadly serpent, just the deadliest you can;
I intend to let him bite me, all the risk I will endure,
Just to prove the sterling value of my wondrous snakebite cure.
Even though an adder bit me, back to life again I'd float;
Snakes are out of date, I tell you, since I've found the antidote.'

Said the scientific person, 'If you really want to die,
Go ahead—but, if you're doubtful, let your sheep-dog have a try.
Get a pair of dogs and try it, let the snake give both a nip;
Give your dog the snakebite mixture, let the other fellow rip;
If he dies and yours survives him, then it proves the thing is good.
Will you fetch your dog and try it?' Johnson rather thought he would.
So he went and fetched his canine, hauled him forward by the throat.
'Stump, old man,' says he, 'we'll show them we've the genwine antidote.'

Both the dogs were duly loaded with the poison-gland's contents;
Johnson gave his dog the mixture, then sat down to wait events.
'Mark,' he said, 'in twenty minutes Stump'll be a-rushing round,
While the other wretched creature lies a corpse upon the ground.'
But, alas for William Johnson! ere they'd watched a half-hour's spell
Stumpy was as dead as mutton, t'other dog was live and well.
And the scientific person hurried off with utmost speed,
Tested Johnson's drug and found it was a deadly poison-weed;
Half a tumbler killed an emu, half a spoonful killed a goat,
All the snakes on earth were harmless to that awful antidote.

Down along the Mooki River, on the overlanders' camp,
Where the serpents are in millions, all of the most deadly stamp,
Wanders, daily, William Johnson, down among those poisonous hordes,
Shooting every stray goanna, calls them 'black and yaller frauds'.
And King Billy, of the Mooki, cadging for the cast-off coat,
Somehow seems to dodge the subject of the snake-bite antidote.

Hay and Hell and Booligal

'You come and see me, boys,' he said;
'You'll find a welcome and a bed
And whisky any time you call;
Although our township hasn't got
The name of quite a lively spot—
You see, I live in Booligal.

'And people have an awful down
Upon the district and the town—
Which worse than hell itself they call;
In fact, the saying far and wide
Along the Riverina side
Is "Hay and Hell and Booligal".

'No doubt it suits 'em very well
To say it's worse than Hay or Hell,
But don't you heed their talk at all;
Of course, there's heat—no one denies—
And sand and dust and stacks of flies,
And rabbits, too, at Booligal.

'But such a pleasant, quiet place,
You never see a stranger's face—
They hardly ever care to call;
The drovers mostly pass it by;
They reckon that they'd rather die
Than spend a night in Booligal.

'The big mosquitoes frighten some—
You'll lie awake to hear 'em hum—
And snakes about the township crawl;
But shearers, when they get their cheque,
They never come along and wreck
The blessed town of Booligal.

'But down in Hay the shearers come
And fill themselves with fighting-rum,
And chase blue devils up the wall,
And fight the snaggers every day,
Until there is the deuce to pay—
There's none of that in Booligal.

'Of course, there isn't much to see—
The billiard-table used to be
The great attraction for us all,
Until some careless, drunken curs
Got sleeping on it in their spurs,
And ruined it, in Booligal.

'Just now there is a howling drought
That pretty near has starved us out—
It never seems to rain at all;
But, if there *should* come any rain,
You couldn't cross the black-soil plain—
You'd have to stop in Booligal.'

'We'd have to stop!' With bated breath
We prayed that both in life and death
Our fate in other lines might fall:
'Oh, send us to our just reward
In Hay or Hell, but, gracious Lord,
Deliver us from Booligal!'

Out of Sight

They held a polo meeting at a little country town,
And all the local sportsmen came to win themselves renown.
There came two strangers with a horse, and I am much afraid
They both belonged to what is called 'the take-you-down brigade'.

They said their horse could jump like fun, and asked an amateur
To ride him in the steeplechase, and told him they were sure,
The last time round, he'd sail away with such a swallow's flight
The rest would never see him go—he'd finish out of sight.

So out he went; and, when folk saw the amateur was up,
Some local genius called the race 'the dude-in-danger cup'.
The horse was known as 'Who's Afraid', by 'Panic' from 'The Fright'
But still his owners told the jock he'd finish out of sight.

And so he did; for 'Who's Afraid', without the least pretence,
Disposed of him by rushing through the very second fence;
And when they ran the last time round the prophecy was right—
For he was in the ambulance, and safely 'out of sight'.

Mulga Bill's Bicycle

'Twas Mulga Bill, from Eaglehawk, that caught the cycling craze;
He turned away the good old horse that served him many days;
He dressed himself in cycling clothes, resplendent to be seen;
He hurried off to town and bought a shining new machine;
And as he wheeled it through the door, with air of lordly pride,
The grinning shop assistant said, 'Excuse me, can you ride?'

'See, here, young man,' said Mulga Bill, 'from Walgett to the sea,
From Conroy's Gap to Castlereagh, there's none can ride like me.
I'm good all round at everything, as everybody knows,
Although I'm not the one to talk—I *hate* a man that blows.
But riding is my special gift, my chiefest, sole delight;
Just ask a wild duck can it swim, a wild cat can it fight.
There's nothing clothed in hair or hide, or built of flesh or steel,

There's nothing walks or jumps, or runs, on axle, hoof, or wheel,
But what I'll sit, while hide will hold and girths and straps are tight:
I'll ride this here two-wheeled concern right straight away at sight.'

'Twas Mulga Bill, from Eaglehawk, that sought his own abode,
That perched above the Dead Man's Creek, beside the mountain road.
He turned the cycle down the hill and mounted for the fray,
But ere he'd gone a dozen yards it bolted clean away.
It left the track, and through the trees, just like a silver streak,
It whistled down the awful slope, towards the Dead Man's Creek.

It shaved a stump by half an inch, it dodged a big white-box:
The very wallaroos in fright went scrambling up the rocks,
The wombats hiding in their caves dug deeper underground,
As Mulga Bill, as white as chalk, sat tight to every bound.
It struck a stone and gave a spring that cleared a fallen tree,
It raced beside a precipice as close as close could be;
And then as Mulga Bill let out one last despairing shriek
It made a leap of twenty feet into the Dead Man's Creek.

'Twas Mulga Bill, from Eaglehawk, that slowly swam ashore:
He said, 'I've had some narrer shaves and lively rides before;
I've rode a wild bull round a yard to win a five pound bet,
But this was the most awful ride that I've encountered yet.
I'll give that two-wheeled outlaw best; it's shaken all my nerve
To feel it whistle through the air and plunge and buck and swerve.
It's safe at rest in Dead Man's Creek, we'll leave it lying still;
A horse's back is good enough henceforth for Mulga Bill.'

With the Cattle

The drought is down on field and flock,
   The river bed is dry;
And we must shift the starving stock
   Before the cattle die.
We muster up with weary hearts
   At breaking of the day,
And turn our heads to foreign parts,
   To take the stock away.
      And it's hunt 'em up and dog 'em,
      And it's get the whip and flog 'em,
For it's weary work is droving when they're dying
         every day;
      By stock routes bare and eaten,
      On dusty roads and beaten,
With half a chance to save their lives we take the
         stock away.

We cannot use the whip for shame
   On beasts that crawl along;
We have to drop the weak and lame,

And try to save the strong;
The wrath of God is on the track,
The drought fiend holds his sway,
With blows and cries and stockwhip crack
We take the stock away.
As they fall we leave them lying,
With the crows to watch them dying,
Grim sextons of the Overland that fasten on their prey;
By the fiery dust storm drifting,
And the mocking mirage shifting,
In heat and drought and hopeless pain we take the stock away.

In dull despair the days go by
With never hope of change,
But every stage we draw more nigh
Towards the mountain range;
And some may live to climb the pass,
And reach the great plateau,
And revel in the mountain grass,
By streamlets fed with snow.
As the mountain wind is blowing
It starts the cattle lowing,
And calling to each other down the dusty long array;
And there speaks a grizzled drover:
'Well, thank God, the worst is over,
The creatures smell the mountain grass that's twenty miles away.'

They press towards the mountain grass,
They look with eager eyes
Along the rugged stony pass,
That slopes towards the skies;
Their feet may bleed from rocks and stones,
But though the blood-drop starts,
They struggle on with stifled groans,
For hope is in their hearts.
And the cattle that are leading,
Though their feet are worn and bleeding,
Are breaking to a kind of run—pull up, and let them go!
For the mountain wind is blowing,
And the mountain grass is growing,
They settle down by running streams ice-cold with melted snow.

The days are done of heat and drought
Upon the stricken plain;
The wind has shifted right about,
And brought the welcome rain;
The river runs with sullen roar,
All flecked with yellow foam,
And we must take the road once more,
To bring the cattle home.
And it's 'Lads! we'll raise a chorus,
There's a pleasant trip before us.'
And the horses bound beneath us as we start them down the track;
And the drovers canter, singing,
Through the sweet green grasses springing,
Towards the far-off mountain land, to bring the cattle back.

Are these the beasts we brought away
That move so lively now?
They scatter off like flying spray
Across the mountain's brow;
And dashing down the rugged range
We hear the stockwhip crack,
Good faith, it is a welcome change
To bring such cattle back.
And it's 'Steady down the lead there!'
And it's 'Let 'em stop and feed there!'
For they're wild as mountain eagles and their sides are all afoam;
But they're settling down already,
And they'll travel nice and steady,
With cheery call and jest and song we fetch the cattle home.

We have to watch them close at night
For fear they'll make a rush,
And break away in headlong flight
Across the open bush;
And by the campfire's cheery blaze,
With mellow voice and strong,
We hear the lonely watchman raise
The Overlander's song:

'Oh! it's when we're done with roving,
With the camping and the droving,
It's homeward down the Bland we'll go, and never more we'll roam';
While the stars shine out above us,
Like the eyes of those who love us—
The eyes of those who watch and wait to greet the cattle home.

The plains are all awave with grass,
The skies are deepest blue;
And leisurely the cattle pass
And feed the long day through;
But when we sight the station gate,
We make the stockwhips crack,
A welcome sound to those who wait
To greet the cattle back:
And through the twilight falling
We hear their voices calling,
As the cattle splash across the ford and churn it into foam;
And the children run to meet us,
And our wives and sweethearts greet us,
Their heroes from the Overland who brought the cattle home.

The Daylight is Dying

The daylight is dying
Away in the west,
The wild birds are flying
In silence to rest;
In leafage and frondage
Where shadows are deep,
They pass to its bondage—
The kingdom of sleep.
And watched in their sleeping
By stars in the height,
They rest in your keeping,
Oh, wonderful night.

When night doth her glories
  Of starshine unfold,
'Tis then that the stories
  Of bushland are told.
Unnumbered I hold them
  In memories bright,
But who could unfold them,
  Or read them aright?
Beyond all denials
  The stars in their glories
The breeze in the myalls
  Are part of these stories.
The waving of grasses,
  The song of the river
That sings as it passes
  For ever and ever,
The hobble chains rattle,
  The calling of birds,
The lowing of cattle
  Must blend with the words.
Without these, indeed, you
  Would find it ere long,
As though I should read you
  The words of a song
That lamely would linger
  When lacking the rune,
The voice of the singer,
  The lilt of the tune.

But, as one half-hearing
  An old-time refrain,
With memory clearing,
  Recalls it again,
These tales, roughly wrought of
  The bush and its ways,
May call back a thought of
  The wandering days,
And, blending with each
  In the mem'ries that throng,
There haply shall reach
  You some echo of song.

Jim Carew

Born of a thoroughbred English race,
  Well proportioned and closely knit,
Neat of figure and handsome face,
  Always ready and always fit,
Hard and wiry of limb and thew,
  That was the ne'er-do-well Jim Carew.

One of the sons of the good old land—
  Many a year since his like was known;
Never a game but he took command,
  Never a sport but he held his own;
Gained at his college a triple blue—
  Good as they make them was Jim Carew.

Came to grief—was it card or horse?
  Nobody asked and nobody cared;
Ship him away to the bush of course,
  Ne'er-do-well fellows are easily spared;
Only of women a tolerable few
  Sorrowed at parting with Jim Carew.

Gentleman Jim on the cattle camp,
  Sitting his horse with an easy grace;
But the reckless living has left its stamp
  In the deep drawn lines of that handsome face,
And a harder look in those eyes of blue:
  Prompt at a quarrel is Jim Carew.

Billy the Lasher was out for gore—
   Twelve-stone navvy with chest of hair,
When he opened out with a hungry roar
   On a ten-stone man it was hardly fair;
But his wife was wise if his face she knew
   By the time you were done with him, Jim Carew.

Gentleman Jim in the stockmen's hut
   Works with them, toils with them, side by side;
As to his past—well, his lips are shut,
   'Gentleman once,' say his mates with pride,
And the wildest Cornstalk can ne'er outdo
   In feats of recklessness, Jim Carew.

What should he live for? A dull despair!
   Drink is his master and drags him down,
Water of Lethe that drowns all care.
   Gentleman Jim has a lot to drown,
And he reigns as king with a drunken crew,
   Sinking to misery, Jim Carew.

Such is the end of the ne'er-do-well—
   Jimmy the Boozer, all down at heel;
But he straightens up when he's asked to tell
   His name and race, and a flash of steel
Still lightens up in those eyes of blue—
   'I am, or—no I *was*—Jim Carew.'

The Swagman's Rest

We buried old Bob where the bloodwoods wave
   At the foot of the Eaglehawk;
We fashioned a cross on the old man's grave,
   For fear that his ghost might walk;
We carved his name on a bloodwood tree,
   With the date of his sad decease,
And in place of 'Died from effects of spree',
   We wrote, 'May he rest in peace'.

For Bob was known on the Overland,
   A regular old bush wag,
Tramping along in the dust and sand,
   Humping his well worn swag.
He would camp for days in the river bed,
   And loiter and 'fish for whales'.
'I'm into the swagman's yard', he said,
   'And I never shall find the rails.'

But he found the rails on that summer night
   For a better place—or worse,
As we watched by turns in the flickering light
   With an old black gin for nurse.

The breeze came in with the scent of pine,
The river sounded clear,
When a change came on, and we saw the sign
That told us the end was near.

But he spoke in a cultured voice and low—
'I fancy they've "sent the route";
I once was an army man, you know,
Though now I'm a drunken brute;
But bury me out where the bloodwoods wave,
And if ever you're fairly stuck,
Just shovel me out of the grave,
And, maybe, I'll bring you luck.

'For I've always heard—' here his voice fell weak,
His strength was well-nigh sped,
He gasped and struggled and tried to speak,
Then fell in a moment—dead.
Thus ended a wasted life and hard,
Of energies misapplied—
Old Bob was out of the 'swagman's yard'
And over the Great Divide.

* * *

The drought came down on the field and flock,
And never a raindrop fell,
Though the tortured moans of the starving stock
Might soften a fiend from hell.
And we thought of the hint that the swagman gave
When he went to the Great Unseen—
We shovelled the skeleton out of the grave
To see what his hint might mean.

We dug where the cross and the graveposts were,
We shovelled away the mould,
When sudden a vein of quartz lay bare
All gleaming with yellow gold.
'Twas a reef with never a fault nor baulk
That ran from the range's crest,
And the richest mine on the Eaglehawk
Is known as 'The Swagman's Rest'.

Under the Shadows of Kiley's Hill

This is the place where they all were bred;
Some of the rafters are standing still;
Now they are scattered and lost and dead,
Every one from the old nest fled,
Out of the shadow of Kiley's Hill.

Better it is that they ne'er came back—
Changes and chances are quickly rung;
Now the old homestead is gone to rack,
Green is the grass on the well-worn track
Down by the gate where the roses clung.

Gone is the garden they kept with care;
Left to decay at its own sweet will,
Fruit trees and flower beds eaten bare,
Cattle and sheep where the roses were,
Under the shadow of Kiley's Hill.

Where are the children that throve and grew
In the old homestead in days gone by?
One is away on the far Barcoo
Watching his cattle the long year through,
Watching them starve in the droughts and die.

One in the town where all cares are rife,
Weary with troubles that cramp and kill,
Fain would be done with the restless strife,
Fain would go back to the old bush life,
Back to the shadow of Kiley's Hill.

One is away on the roving quest,
Seeking his share of the golden spoil,
Out in the wastes of the trackless west,
Wandering ever he gives the best
Of his years and strength to the hopeless toil.

What of the parents? That unkept mound
Shows where they slumber united still;
Rough is their grave, but they sleep as sound
Out on the range as on holy ground,
Under the shadow of Kiley's Hill.

The Wind's Message

There came a whisper down the Bland* between the dawn and dark,
Above the tossing of the pines, above the river's flow;
It stirred the boughs of giant gums and stalwart ironbark;
It drifted where the wild ducks played amid the swamps below;
It brought a breath of mountain air from off the hills of pine,
A scent of eucalyptus trees in honey-laden bloom;
And drifting, drifting far away along the southern line
It caught from leaf and grass and fern a subtle strange perfume.

It reached the toiling city folk, but few there were that heard—
The rattle of their busy life had choked the whisper down;
And some but caught a fresh-blown breeze with scent of pine that stirred
A thought of blue hills far away beyond the smoky town;
And others heard the whisper pass, but could not understand
The magic of the breeze's breath that set their hearts aglow,
Nor how the roving wind could bring across the Overland
A sound of voices silent now and songs of long ago.

But some that heard the whisper clear were filled with vague unrest;

** The Bland is a county in the southern districts of New South Wales.*

The breeze had brought its message home, they could not fixed abide;
Their fancies wandered all the day towards the blue hills' breast,
Towards the sunny slopes that lie along the riverside,
The mighty rolling western plains are very fair to see,
Where waving to the passing breeze the silver myalls stand,
But fairer are the giant hills, all rugged though they be,
From which the two great rivers rise that run along the Bland.

Oh! rocky range and rugged spur and river running clear,
That swings around the sudden bends with swirl of snow-white foam,
Though we, your sons, are far away, we sometimes seem to hear
The message that the breezes bring to call the wanderers home.
The mountain peaks are white with snow that feeds a thousand rills,
Along the river banks the maize grows tall on virgin land,
And we shall live to see once more those sunny southern hills,
And strike once more the bridle track that leads along the Bland.

Pioneers

They came of bold and roving stock that would not fixed abide;
They were the sons of field and flock since e'er they learned to ride;
We may not hope to see such men in these degenerate years
As those explorers of the bush—the brave old pioneers.

'Twas they who rode the trackless bush in heat and storm and drought;
'Twas they that heard the master-word that called them further out;
'Twas they that followed up the trail the mountain cattle made
And pressed across the mighty range where now their bones are laid.

But now the times are dull and slow, the brave old days are dead
When hardy bushmen started out, and forced their way ahead
By tangled scrub and forests grim towards the unknown west,
And spied the far-off promised land from off the ranges' crest.

Oh! ye, that sleep in lonely graves by far-off ridge and plain,
We drink to you in silence now as Christmas comes again,
The men who fought the wilderness through rough, unsettled years—
The founders of our nation's life, the brave old pioneers.

Brumby's Run

Brumby is the Aboriginal word for a wild horse.

It lies beyond the Western Pines
Beneath the sinking sun,
And not a survey mark defines
The bounds of 'Brumby's Run'.

On odds and ends of mountain land,
On tracks of range and rock
Where no one else can make a stand
Old Brumby rears his stock.

A wild, unhandled lot they are
Of every shape and breed.
They venture out 'neath moon and star
Along the flats to feed;

But, when the dawn makes pink the sky
And steals along the plain,
The Brumby horses turn and fly
Back to the hills again.

The traveller by the mountain-track
May hear their hoof-beats pass,
And catch a glimpse of brown and black
Dim shadows on the grass.

The eager stockhorse pricks his ears,
And lifts his head on high
In wild excitement, when he hears
The Brumby mob go by.

Old Brumby asks no price or fee
O'er all his wide domains:
The man who yards his stock is free
To keep them for his pains.

So, off to scour the mountain-side
With eager eyes aglow,
To strongholds where the wild mobs hide
The gully-rakers go.

A rush of horses through the trees,
A red shirt making play;
A sound of stockwhips on the breeze,
They vanish far away!

Ah, me! before our day is done
We long with bitter pain
To ride once more on Brumby's Run
And yard his mob again.

'Shouting' for a Camel

It was over at Coolgardie that a mining speculator,
Who was going down the township just to make a bit o'chink,
Went off to hire a camel from a camel propagator,
And the Afghan said he'd lend it if he'd stand the beast a drink.
Yes, the only price he asked him was to stand the beast a drink.
He was cheap, very cheap, as the dromedaries go.

So the mining speculator made the bargain, proudly thinking
He had bested old Mahomet, he had done him in the eye.
Then he clambered on the camel, and while the beast was drinking
He explained with satisfaction to the miners standing by
That 'twas cheap, very cheap, as the dromedaries go.

But the camel kept on drinking and he filled his hold with water,
And the more he had inside him yet the more he seemed to need;
For he drank it by the gallon, and his girths grew taut and tauter,
And the miners muttered softly, 'Yes he's very dry indeed!
But he's cheap, very cheap, as the dromedaries go.'

So he drank up twenty buckets—it was weird to watch him suck it,
(And the market price for water was per bucket half-a-crown)
Till the speculator stopped him, saying, 'Not another bucket—
If I give him any more there'll be a famine in the town.
Take him back to old Mahomet, and I'll tramp it through the town.'
He was cheap, very cheap, as the speculators go.

There's a moral to this story—in your hat you ought to paste it—
Be careful whom you shout for when a camel is about,
And there's plenty human camels who, before they'll see you waste it,
Will drink up all your earnings if you're fool enough to shout;
If you chance to strike a camel when you're fool enough to shout,
You'll be cheap, very cheap, as the speculators go.

Song of the Artesian Water

Now the stock have started dying, for the Lord has sent a drought;
But we're sick of prayers and Providence—we're going to do without;
With the derricks up above us and the solid earth below,
We are waiting at the lever for the word to let her go.
   Sinking down, deeper down,
   Oh, we'll sink it deeper down:
As the drill is plugging downward at a thousand feet of level,
If the Lord won't send us water, oh, we'll get it from the devil;
Yes, we'll get it from the devil deeper down.

Now, our engine's built in Glasgow by a very canny Scot,
And he marked it twenty horse-power, but he don't know what is what:
When Canadian Bill is firing with the sun-dried gidgee logs,
She can equal thirty horses and a score or so of dogs.
   Sinking down, deeper down,
   Oh, we're going deeper down:
If we fail to get the water then it's ruin to the squatter,
For the drought is on the station and the weather's growing hotter,
But we're bound to get the water deeper down.

But the shaft has started caving and the sinking's very slow,
And the yellow rods are bending in the water down below,
And the tubes are always jamming and they can't be made to shift
Till we nearly burst the engine with a forty horse-power lift.
   Sinking down, deeper down,
   Oh, we're going deeper down:
Though the shaft is always caving, and the tubes are always jamming,
Yet we'll fight our way to water while the stubborn drill is ramming—
While the stubborn drill is ramming deeper down.

But there's no artesian water—though we've passed three thousand feet,
And the contract price is growing and the boss is nearly beat.
But it must be down beneath us, and it's down we've got to go,
Though she's bumping on the solid rock four thousand feet below.
   Sinking down, deeper down,
   Oh, we're going deeper down:
And it's time they heard us knocking on the roof of Satan's dwellin';
But we'll get artesian water if we cave the roof of hell in—
Oh! we'll get artesian water deeper down.

But it's hark! the whistle's blowing with a wild, exultant blast,
And the boys are madly cheering, for they've struck the flow at last,

And it's rushing up the tubing from four thousand feet below
Till its spouts above the casing in a million-gallon flow.
   And it's down, deeper down,
   Oh, it comes from deeper down;
It is flowing, ever flowing, in a free, unstinted measure
From the silent hidden places where the old earth hides her treasure—
Where the old earth hides her treasure deeper down.

And it's clear away the timber, and it's let the water run:
How it glimmers in the shadow, how it flashes in the sun!
By the silent belts of timber, by the miles of blazing plain
It is bringing hope and comfort to the thirsty land again.
   Flowing down, further down;
   It is flowing further down
To the tortured thirsty cattle, bringing gladness in its going;
Through the droughty days of summer it is flowing, ever flowing—
It is flowing, ever flowing, further down.

The Story of Mongrel Grey

This is the story the stockman told,
On the cattle camp, when the stars were bright;
The moon rose up like a globe of gold
And flooded the plain with her mellow light.
We watched the cattle till dawn of day
And he told me the story of Mongrel Grey.

'He was a knock-about station hack,
Spurred and walloped, and banged and beat;
Ridden all day with a sore on his back,
Left all night with nothing to eat.
That was a matter of everyday—
Common occurrence for Mongrel Grey.

'Pr'aps we'd have sold him, but someone heard
He was bred out back on a flooded run,
Where he learned to swim like a water bird,
Midnight or midday were all as one.
In the flooded ground he could find his way,
Nothing could puzzle old Mongrel Grey.
' 'Tis a special gift that some horses learn,
When the floods are out they will splash along
In girth-deep water, and twist and turn
From hidden channel and billabong.
Never mistaking the road to go,
For a man may guess—but the horses *know*.

'I was camping out with my youngest son
—Bit of a nipper just learnt to speak—
In an empty hut on the lower run,
Shooting and fishing in Conroy's Creek.
The youngster toddled about all day,
And with our horses was Mongrel Grey.

'All of a sudden the flood came down
Fresh from the hills with the mountain rain,
Roaring and eddying, rank and brown,
Over the flats and across the plain.
Rising and falling—fall of night—
Nothing but water appeared in sight!
' 'Tis a nasty place when the floods are out,
Even in daylight, for all around

Channels and billabongs twist about,
Stretching for miles in the flooded ground.
And to move was a hopeless thing to try
In the dark, with the water just racing by.

'I had to try it. I heard a roar,
And the wind swept down with the blinding rain;
And the water rose till it reached the floor
Of our highest room, and t'was very plain
The way the water was sweeping down
We must shift for the highlands at once, or drown.

'Off to the stable I splashed, and found
The horses shaking with cold and fright;
I led them down to the lower ground,
But never a yard they swam that night!
They reared and snorted and turned away,
And none would face it but Mongrel Grey.

'I bound the child on the horse's back,
And we started off with a prayer to heaven,
Through the rain and wind and the pitchy black,
For I knew that the instinct God has given
To guide His creatures by night and day
Would lead the footsteps of Mongrel Grey.

'He struck deep water at once and swam—
I swam beside him and held his mane—
Till we touched the bank of the broken dam
In shallow water—then off again,
Swimming in darkness across the flood,
Rank with the smell of the drifting mud.

'He turned and twisted across and back,
Choosing the places to wade and swim,
Picking the safest and shortest track,
The pitchy darkness was clear to him.
Did he strike the crossing by sight or smell?
The Lord that led him alone could tell!

'He dodged the timber whene'er he could,
But the timber brought us to grief at last;
I was partly stunned by a log of wood,
That struck my head as it drifted past;
And I lost my grip of the brave old grey,
And in half a second he swept away.

'I reached a tree, where I had to stay,
And did a perish for two days hard;
And lived on water—but Mongrel Grey,
He walked right into the homestead yard
At dawn next morning, and grazed around,
With the child on top of him safe and sound.

'We keep him now for the wife to ride,
Nothing too good for him now of course;
Never a whip on his fat old hide,
For she owes the child to that old grey horse.
And not Old Tyson himself could pay,
The purchase money of Mongrel Grey.'

Rio Grande's Last Race

Now this was what Macpherson told
  While waiting in the stand;
A reckless rider, over-bold,
The only man with hands to hold
  The rushing Rio Grande.

He said, 'This day I bid good-bye
  To bit and bridle rein,
To ditches deep and fences high,
For I have dreamed a dream, and I
  Shall never ride again.

'I dreamt last night I rode this race
  That I to-day must ride,
And cant'ring down to take my place
I saw full many an old friend's face
  Come stealing to my side.

'Dead men on horses long since dead,
  They clustered on the track;
The champions of the days long fled,
They moved around with noiseless tread—
  Bay, chestnut, brown, and black.

'And one man on a big grey steed
  Rode up and waved his hand;
Said he, "We help a friend in need,
And we have come to give a lead
  To you and Rio Grande.

' "For you must give the field the slip,
  So never draw the rein,
But keep him moving with the whip,
And if he falter—set your lip
  And rouse him up again.

' "But when you reach the big stone wall,
  Put down your bridle hand
And let him sail—he cannot fall—
But don't you interfere at all;
  You trust old Rio Grande."

'We started, and in front we showed,
  The big horse running free:
Right fearlessly and game he strode,
And by my side those dead men rode
  Whom no one else could see.

'As silently as flies a bird,
  They rode on either hand;
At every fence I plainly heard
The phantom leader give the word,
  "Make room for Rio Grande!"

'I spurred him on to get the lead,
  I chanced full many a fall;
But swifter still each phantom steed
Kept with me, and at racing speed
  We reached the big stone wall.

'And there the phantoms on each side
  Drew in and blocked his leap;
"Make room! make room!" I loudly cried,
But right in front they seemed to ride—
  I cursed them in my sleep.

'He never flinched, he faced it game,
  He struck it with his chest,
And every stone burst out in flame,
And Rio Grande and I became
  As phantoms with the rest.

'And then I woke, and for a space
  All nerveless did I seem;
For I have ridden many a race,
But never one at such a pace
  As in that fearful dream.

'And I am sure as man can be
  That out upon the track,
Those phantoms that men cannot see
Are waiting now to ride with me,
  And I shall not come back.

'For I must ride the dead men's race,
  And follow their command;
'Twere worse than death, the foul disgrace
If I should fear to take my place
  To-day on Rio Grande.'

He mounted, and a jest he threw,
  With never sign of gloom;
But all who heard the story knew
That Jack Macpherson, brave and true,
  Was going to his doom.

They started, and the big black steed
  Came flashing past the stand;
All single-handed in the lead
He strode along at racing speed,
  The mighty Rio Grande.

But on his ribs the whalebone stung,
  A madness it did seem!
And soon it rose on every tongue
That Jack Macpherson rode among
  The creatures of his dream.

He looked to left and looked to right,
As though men rode beside;
And Rio Grande, with foam-flecks white,
Raced at his jumps in headlong flight
And cleared them in his stride.

But when they reached the big stone wall,
Down went the bridle-hand,
And loud we heard Macpherson call,
'Make room, or half the field will fall!
Make room for Rio Grande!'

'He's down! he's down!' And horse and man
Lay quiet side by side!
No need the pallid face to scan,
We knew with Rio Grande he ran
The race the dead men ride.

The Ballad of the Calliope

By the far Samoan shore,
Where the league-long rollers pour
All the wash of the Pacific on the coral-guarded bay,
Riding lightly at their ease,
In the calm of tropic seas,
The three great nations' warships at their anchors proudly lay.

Riding lightly, head to wind,
With the coral reefs behind,
Three Germans and three Yankee ships were mirrored in the blue;
And on one ship unfurled
Was the flag that rules the world—
For on the old *Calliope* the flag of England flew.

When the gentle off-shore breeze,
That had scarcely stirred the trees,
Dropped down to utter stillness, and the glass began to fall,
Away across the main
Lowered the coming hurricane,
And far away to seaward hung the cloud wrack like a pall.

If the word had passed around,
'Let us move to safer ground;
Let us steam away to seaward'—then this tale were not to tell!
But each Captain seemed to say
If the others stay, I stay!'
And they lingered at their moorings till the shades of evening fell.

Then the cloud-wrack neared them fast,
And there came a sudden blast,
And the hurricane came leaping down a thousand miles of main!

Like a lion on its prey,
Leapt the storm fiend on the bay,
And the vessels shook and shivered as their cable felt the strain.

As the surging seas came by,
That were running mountains high,
The vessels started dragging, drifting slowly to the lee;
And the darkness of the night
Hid the coral reefs from sight,
And the Captains dared not risk the chance to grope their way to sea.

In the dark they dared not shift!
They were forced to wait and drift;
All hands stood by uncertain would the anchors hold or no.
But the men on deck could see
If a chance of hope might be—
There was little chance of safety for the men who were below.

Through that long, long night of dread,
While the storm raged overhead,
They were waiting by their engines, with the furnace fires aroar.
So they waited, staunch and true,
Though they knew, and well they knew,
They must drown like rats imprisoned if the vessel touched the shore.

When the grey dawn broke at last,
And the long, long night was past,
While the hurricane redoubled, lest its prey should steal away,
On the rocks, all smashed and strewn,
Were the German vessels thrown,
While the Yankees, swamped and helpless, drifted shorewards down the bay.

Then at last spoke Captain Kane,
All our anchors are in vain,
And the Germans and the Yankees they have drifted to the lee!
Cut the cables at the bow!
We must trust the engines now!
Give her steam, and let her have it, lads, we'll fight her out to sea!'

And the answer came with cheers
From the stalwart engineers,
From the grim and grimy firemen at the furnaces below;
And above the sullen roar
Of the breakers on the shore
Came the throbbing of the engines as they laboured to and fro.

If the strain should find a flaw,
Should a bolt or rivet draw,
Then—God help them! for the vessel were a plaything in the tide!
With a face of honest cheer,
Quoth an English engineer,
'I will answer for the engines that were built on old Thames side!

'For the stays and stanchions taut,
For the rivets truly wrought,
For the valves that fit their faces as a glove should fit the hand.
Give her every ounce of power,
If we make a knot an hour
Then it's way enough to steer her and we'll drive her from the land.'

Like a foam flake tossed and thrown,
She could barely hold her own,
While the other ships all helplessly were drifting to the lee.
Through the smother and the rout
The *Calliope* steamed out—
And they cheered her from the *Trenton* that was foundering in the sea.

Aye! drifting shoreward there,
All helpless as they were,
Their vessel hurled upon the reefs as weed ashore is hurled.
Without a thought of fear
The Yankees raised a cheer—
A cheer that English-speaking folk should echo round the world.

Saltbush Bill's Second Fight

The news came down on the Castlereagh, and went to the world at large,
That twenty thousand travelling sheep, with Saltbush Bill in charge,
Were drifting down from a dried-out run to ravage the Castlereagh;
And the squatters swore when they heard the news, and wished they were well away:
For the name and the fame of Saltbush Bill were over the country side
For the wonderful way that he fed his sheep, and the dodges and tricks he tried.
He would lose his way on a Main Stock Route, and stray to the squatters' grass;
He would come to the run with the boss away, and swear he had leave to pass;
And back of all and behind it all, as well the squatters knew,
If he had to fight, he would fight all day, so long as his sheep got through:

But this is the story of Stingy Smith, the owner of Hard Times Hill,
And the way that he chanced on a fighting man to reckon with Saltbush Bill.

* * *

'Twas Stingy Smith on his stockyard sat, and prayed for an early Spring,
When he stared at sight of a clean-shaved tramp, who walked with a jaunty swing;
For a clean-shaved tramp with a jaunty walk a-swinging along the track
Is as rare a thing as a feathered frog on the desolate roads out back.
So the tramp he made for the travellers' hut, and asked could he camp the night;
But Stingy Smith had a bright idea, and he said to him, 'Can you fight?'
'Why, what's the game?' said the clean-shaved tramp, as he looked at him up and down—
'If you want a battle, get off that fence, and I'll kill you for half-a-crown!
But, Boss, you'd better not fight with me, it wouldn't be fair nor right;
I'm Stiffener Joe, from the Rocks Brigade, and I killed a man in a fight:
I served two years for it, fair and square, and now I'm a trampin' back,
To look for a peaceful quiet life away on the outside track—'
'Oh, it's not myself, but a drover chap,' said Stingy Smith with glee;
'A bullying fellow, called Saltbush Bill—and you are the man for me.
He's on the road with his hungry sheep, and he's certain to raise a row,
For he's bullied the whole of the Castlereagh till he's got them under cow—
Just pick a quarrel and raise a fight, and leather him good and hard,
And I'll take good care that his wretched sheep don't wander half a yard.
It's a five-pound job if you belt him well—do anything short of kill,
For there isn't a beak on the Castlereagh will fine you for Saltbush Bill.'

'I'll take the job,' said the fighting man; 'and hot as this cove appears,
He'll stand no chance with a bloke like me, what's lived on the game for years;
For he's maybe learnt in a boxing school, and sparred for a round or so,
But I've fought all hands in a ten-foot ring each night in a travelling show;
They earned a pound if they stayed three rounds, and they tried for it every night—
In a ten-foot ring! Oh, that's the game that teaches a bloke to fight,
For they'd rush and clinch, it was Dublin Rules, and we drew no colour line;
And they all tried hard for to earn the pound, but they got no pound of mine:
If I saw no chance in the opening round I'd slog at their wind, and wait
Till an opening came—and it *always* came—and I settled 'em, sure as fate;
Left on the ribs and right on the jaw—and, when the chance comes, *make sure!*
And it's there a professional bloke like me gets home on an amateur:
For it's my experience every day. and I make no doubt it's yours,
That a third-class pro is an over-match for the best of the amateurs—'
'Oh, take your swag to the travellers' hut,' said Smith, 'for you waste your breath;
You've a first-class chance, if you lose the fight, of talking your man to death.
I'll tell the cook you're to have your grub, and see that you eat your fill,
And come to the scratch all fit and well to leather this Saltbush Bill.'

* * *

'Twas Saltbush Bill, and his travelling sheep were wending their weary way
On the Main Stock Route, through the Hard Times Run, on their six-mile stage a day;
And he strayed a mile from the Main Stock Route, and started to feed along,
And, when Stingy Smith came up, Bill said that the Route was surveyed wrong;
And he tried to prove that the sheep had rushed and strayed from their camp at night,
But the fighting man he kicked Bill's dog, and of course that meant a fight:
So they sparred and fought, and they shifted ground, and never a sound was heard
But the thudding fists on their brawny ribs, and the seconds' muttered word,
Till the fighting man shot home his left on the ribs with a mighty clout,
And his right flashed up with a half-arm blow—and Saltbush Bill 'went out'.
He fell face down, and towards the blow; and their hearts with fear were filled,
For he lay as still as a fallen tree, and they thought that he must be killed.

So Stingy Smith and the fighting man, they lifted him from the ground,
And sent to home for a brandy flask, and they slowly fetched him round;
But his head was bad, and his jaw was hurt—in fact, he could scarcely speak—
So they let him spell till he got his wits, and he camped on the run for a week,
While the travelling sheep went here and there, wherever they liked to stray,
Till Saltbush Bill was fit once more for the track to the Castlereagh.

Then Stingy Smith he wrote a note, and gave to the fighting man:
'Twas writ to the boss of the neighbouring run, and thus the missive ran:
'The man with this is a fighting man, one Stiffener Joe by name;
He came near murdering Saltbush Bill, and I found it a costly game:
But it's worth your while to employ the chap, for there isn't the slightest doubt
You'll have no trouble from Saltbush Bill while this man hangs about—'
But an answer came by the next week's mail, with news that might well appal:
'The man you sent with a note is not a fighting man at all!
He has shaved his beard, and has cut his hair, but I spotted him at a look;
He is Tom Devine, who has worked for years for Saltbush Bill as cook.
Bill coached him up in the fighting yarn, and taught him the tale by rote,
And they shammed to fight, and they got your grass and divided your five-pound note.
'Twas a clean take-in, and you'll find it wise—'twill save you a lot of pelf—
When next you're hiring a fighting man, just fight him a round yourself.'

And the teamsters out on the Castlereagh, when they meet with a week of rain,
And the waggon sinks to its axle-tree, deep down in the black soil plain,
When the bullocks wade in a sea of mud, and strain at the load of wool,
And the cattle dogs at the bullocks' heels are biting to make them pull,
When the offside driver flays the team, and curses them while he flogs,
And the air is thick with the language used, and the clamour of men and dogs—
The teamsters say, as they pause to rest and moisten each hairy throat,
They wish they could swear like Stingy Smith when he read that neighbour's note.

By the Grey Gulf-water

Far to the northward there lies a land,
  A wonderful land that the winds blow over,
And none may fathom nor understand
  The charm it holds for the restless rover;
A great grey chaos—a land half made,
  Where endless space is and no life stirreth;
And the soul of a man will recoil afraid
  From the sphinx-like visage that Nature weareth.
But old Dame Nature, though scornful, craves
  Her dole of death and her share of slaughter;
Many indeed are the nameless graves
  Where her victims sleep by the Grey Gulf-water.

Slowly and slowly those grey streams glide,
  Drifting along with a languid motion,
Lapping the reed beds on either side,
  Wending their way to the Northern Ocean.
Grey are the plains where the emus pass
  Silent and slow, with their staid demeanour;
Over the dead men's graves the grass
  Maybe is waving a trifle greener.
Down in the world where men toil and spin
  Dame Nature smiles as man's hand has taught her;
Only the dead men her smiles can win
  In the great lone land by the Grey Gulf-water.

For the strength of man is an insect's strength,
  In the face of that mighty plain and river,
And the life of a man is a moment's length
  To the life of the stream that will run for ever.
And so it cometh they take no part
  In a small-world worries; each hardy rover
Rideth abroad and is light of heart,
  With the plains around and the blue sky over.
And up in the heavens the brown lark sings
  The songs that the strange wild land has taught her;
Full of thanksgiving her sweet song rings—
  And I wish I were back by the Grey Gulf-water.

Saltbush Bill's Gamecock

'Twas Saltbush Bill, with his travelling sheep, was making his way to town;
He crossed them over the Hard Times Run, and he came to the Take 'Em Down;
He counted through at the boundary gate, and camped at the drafting yard:
For Stingy Smith, of the Hard Times Run, had hunted him rather hard.
He bore no malice to Stingy Smith—'twas simply the hand of fate
That caused his wagon to swerve aside and shatter old Stingy's gate;
And, being only the hand of fate, it follows, without a doubt,
It wasn't the fault of Saltbush Bill that Stingy's sheep got out.
So Saltbush Bill, with an easy heart, prepared for what might befall,
Commenced his stages on Take 'Em Down, the station of Rooster Hall.

'Tis strange how often the men out back will take to some curious craft,
Some ruling passion to keep their thoughts away from the overdraft;
And Rooster Hall, of the Take 'Em Down, was widely known to fame
As breeder of champion fighting cocks—his *forte* was the British Game.
The passing stranger within his gates that camped with old Rooster Hall
Was forced to talk about fowls all night, or else not talk at all.
Though droughts should come, and though sheep should die, his fowls were his sole delight;
He left his shed in the flood of work to watch two gamecocks fight.
He held in scorn the Australian Game, that long-legged child of sin;
In a desperate fight, with the steel-tipped spurs, the British Game must win!
The Australian bird was a mongrel bird, with a touch of the jungle cock;
The want of breeding must find him out, when facing the English stock;
For British breeding, and British pluck, must triumph it over all—
And that was the root of the simple creed that governed old Rooster Hall.

• • •

'Twas Saltbush Bill to the station rode ahead of his travelling sheep,
And sent a message to Rooster Hall that wakened him out of his sleep
A crafty message that fetched him out, and hurried him as he came—
'A drover has an Australian bird to match with your British Game.'
'Twas done, and done in a half a trice; a five-pound note aside;
Old Rooster Hall, with his champion bird, and the drover's bird untried.
'Steel spurs, of course?' said old Rooster Hall; 'you'll need 'em, without a doubt!'
'You stick the spurs on your bird,' said Bill! 'but mine fights best without.'

'Fights best without?' said old Rooster Hall; 'he can't fight best unspurred!
You must be crazy!' But Saltbush Bill said, 'Wait till you see my bird!'
So Rooster Hall to his fowlyard went, and quickly back he came,
Bearing a clipt and a shaven cock, the pride of his English Game.
With an eye as fierce as an eaglehawk, and a crow like a trumpet call,

He strutted about on the garden walk, and cackled at Rooster Hall.
Then Rooster Hall sent off a boy with word to his cronies two,
McCrae (the boss of the Black Police) and Father Donahoo.
Full many a cockfight old McCrae had held in his empty Court,
With Father D. as a picker-up—a regular all-round Sport!
They got the message of Rooster Hall, and down to his run they came,
Prepared to scoff at the drover's bird, and to bet on the English Game;
They hied them off to the drover's camp, while Saltbush rode before—
Old Rooster Hall was a blithesome man, when he thought of the treat in store.
They reached the camp, where the drover's cook, with countenance all serene,
Was boiling beef in an iron pot, but never a fowl was seen.

'Take off the beef from the fire,' said Bill, 'and wait till you see the fight;
There's something fresh for the bill-of-fare—there's game-fowl stew to-night!
For Mister Hall has a fighting cock, all feathered and clipped and spurred;
And he's fetched him here, for a bit of sport, to fight our Australian bird.
I've made a match that our pet will win, though he's hardly a fighting cock,
But he's game enough, and it's many a mile that he's tramped with the travelling stock.'
The cook he banged on a saucepan lid; and, soon as the sound was heard,
Under the dray, in the shadows hid, a something moved and stirred:
A great tame Emu strutted out. Said Saltbush, 'Here's our bird!'
But Rooster Hall, and his cronies two, drove home without a word.

The passing stranger within his gates that camps with old Rooster Hall
Must talk about something else than fowls, if he wishes to talk at all.
For the record lies in the local Court, and filed in its deepest vault,
That Peter Hall, of the Take 'Em Down, was tried for a fierce assault
On a stranger man, who, in all good faith, and prompted by what he heard,
Had asked old Hall if a British Game could beat an Australian bird;
And old McCrae, who was on the Bench, as soon as the case was tried,
Remarked, 'Discharged with a clean discharge—the assault was justified!'

A Disqualified Jockey's Story

You see, the thing was this way—there was me,
That rode Panoppoly, the Splendor mare,
And Ikey Chambers on the Iron Dook,
And Smith, the half-caste rider, on Regret,
And that long bloke from Wagga—him what rode
Veronikew, the Snowy River horse.
Well, none of them had chances—not a chance
Among the lot, unless the rest fell dead
Or wasn't trying—for a blind man's dog
Could see Enchantress was a certain cop,
And all the books was layin' six to four.

They brought her out to show our lot the road,
Or so they said; but, then, Gord's truth! you know,
You can't believe 'em, though they took an oath
On forty Bibles that they'd tell the truth.
But anyhow, an amateur was up
On this Enchantress, and so Ike and me,

We thought that we might frighten him a bit
By asking if he minded riding rough—
'Oh, not at all,' says he, 'oh, not at all!
I learnt at Robbo Park, and if it comes
To bumping I'm your Moses! Strike me blue!'

Says he, 'I'll bump you over either rail,
The inside rail or outside—which you choose
Is good enough for me'—which settled Ike;
For he was shaky since he near got killed
From being sent a buster on the rail,
When some chap bumped his horse and fetched him
down
At Stony Bridge, so Ikey thought it best
To leave this bloke alone, and I agreed.

So all the books was layin' six to four
Against the favourite, and the amateur
Was walking this Enchantress up and down,
And me and Smithy backed him; for we thought
We might as well get something for ourselves,
Because we knew our horses couldn't win.
But Ikey wouldn't back him for a bob;
Because he said he reckoned he was stiff,
And all the books was layin' six to four.

Well, anyhow, before the start, the news
Got round that this here amateur was stiff,
And our good stuff was blued, and all the books
Was in it, and the prices lengthened out,
And every book was bustin' of his throat,
And layin' five to one the favourite.
So there was we that couldn't win ourselves,
And this here amateur that wouldn't try,
And all the books was layin' five to one.

So Smithy says to me, 'You take a hold
Of that there moke of yours, and round the turn
Come up behind Enchantress with the whip
And let her have it; that long bloke and me
Will wait ahead, and when she comes to us
We'll pass her on and belt her down the straight,
And Ikey'll flog her home, because his boss
Is judge and steward and the Lord knows what,
And so he won't be touched—and, as for us,
We'll swear we only hit her by mistake!'
And all the books was layin' five to one.

Well, off we went, and comin' to the turn
I saw the amateur was holding back
And poking into every hole he could
To get her blocked, and so I pulled behind
And drew the whip and dropped it on the mare—
I let her have it twice, and then she shot
Ahead of me, and Smithy opened out
And let her up beside him on the rails,
And kept her there a-beltin' her like smoke
Until she struggled past him pullin' hard
And came to Ike; but Ikey drew his whip
And hit her on the nose and sent her back
And won the race himself—for, after all,
It seems he had a fiver on the Dook
And never told us—so our stuff was lost.
And then they had us up for ridin' foul,
And warned us off the tracks for twelve months
each,
To get our livin' any way we could;
But Ikey wasn't touched, because his boss
Was judge and steward and the Lord knows what.

But Mister—if you'll lend us half-a-crown,
I know three certain winners at the Park—
Three certain cops as no one knows but me;
And—thank you, Mister, come an' have a beer
(I always like a beer about this time)...
Well, so long, Mister, till we meet again.

T.Y.S.O.N.

Across the Queensland border line
The mobs of cattle go;
They travel down in sun and shine
On dusty stage, and slow.
The drovers, riding slowly on
To let the cattle spread,
Will say: 'Here's one old landmark gone,
For old man Tyson's dead.'

What tales there'll be in every camp
By men that Tyson knew!
The swagmen, meeting on the tramp,
Will yarn the long day through,
And tell of how he passed as 'Brown',
And fooled the local men:
'But not for me—I struck the town,
And passed the message further down;
That's T.Y.S.O.N.!'

There stands a little country town
Beyond the border line,
Where dusty roads go up and down,
And banks with pubs combine.
A stranger came to cash a cheque—
Few were the words he said—
A handkerchief about his neck,
An old hat on his head.

A long grey stranger, eagle-eyed—
'Know me? Of course you do?'
'It's not my work,' the boss replied,
'To know such tramps as you.'
'Well, look here, Mister, don't be flash,'
Replied the stranger then,
'I never care to make a splash,
I'm simple, but I've got the cash;
I'm T.Y.S.O.N.!'

But in that last great drafting-yard,
Where Peter keeps the gate,
And souls of sinners find it barred,
And go to meet their fate,
There's one who ought to enter in
For good deeds done on earth,
One who from Peter's self must win
That meed of sterling worth.

Not to the strait and narrow gate
Reserved for wealthy men,
But to the big gate, opened wide,
The grizzled figure, eagle-eyed,
Will saunter up—and then
Old Peter'll say: 'Let's pass him through;
There's many a thing he used to do,
Good-hearted things that no one knew;
That's T.Y.S.O.N.'

James Tyson (1819–98) was a well-known Australian pastoralist.

The Reverend Mullineux

I'd reckon his weight at eight-stun-eight,
  And his height at five-foot-two,
With a face as plain as an eight-day clock
And a walk as brisk as a bantam-cock—
  Game as a bantam, too,
Hard and wiry and full of steam,
That's the boss of the English Team,
  Reverend Mullineux!

Makes no row when the game gets rough—
  None of your 'Strike me blue!'
'Yous wants smacking across the snout!'—
Plays like a gentleman out-and-out,
  Same as he ought to do.
'Kindly remove from off my face!'
That's the way that he states his case,
  Reverend Mullineux.

Kick! He can kick like an army mule—
  Run like a kangaroo!
Hard to get by as a lawyer-plant,
Tackles his man like a bull-dog ant—
  Fetches him over too!
Didn't the public cheer and shout
Watchin' him chuckin' big blokes about,
  Reverend Mullineux!

Scrimmage was packed on his prostrate form,
  Somehow the ball got through—
Who was it tackled our big half-back,
Flinging him down like an empty sack,
  Right on our goal-line too?
Who but the man that we thought was dead,
Down with a score of 'em on his head,
  Reverend Mullineux.

The First Surveyor

'The opening of the railway line!—the Governor and all!
With flags and banners down the street, a banquet and a ball.
Hark to 'em at the station now! They're raising cheer on cheer!
"The man who brought the railway through—our friend the engineer!"

'They cheer *his* pluck and enterprise and engineering skill!
'Twas my old husband found the pass behind that big Red Hill.
Before the engineer was grown we settled with our stock
Behind that great big mountain chain, a line of range and rock—
A line that kept us starving there in weary weeks of drought,
With ne'er a track across the range to let the cattle out.

' 'Twas then, with horses starved and weak and scarcely fit to crawl,
My husband went to find a way across that rocky wall.
He vanished in the wilderness, God knows where he was gone,
He hunted till his food gave out, but still he battled on.
His horses strayed—'twas well they did—they made towards the grass,
And down behind that big red hill they found an easy pass.

'He followed up and blazed the trees, to show the safest track,
Then drew his belt another hole and turned and started back.
His horses died—just one pulled through with nothing much to spare;
God bless the beast that brought him home, the old white Arab mare!
We drove the cattle through the hills, along the new-found way,
And this was our first camping-ground—just where I live to-day.

'Then others came across the range and built the township here,
And then there came the railway line and this young engineer.
He drove about with tents and traps, a cook to cook his meals,
A bath to wash himself at night, a chain-man at his heels.
And that was all the pluck and skill for which he's cheered and praised,
For after all he took the track, the same my husband blazed!

'My poor old husband, dead and gone with never feast nor cheer;
He's buried by the railway line!—I wonder can he hear
When down the very track he marked, and close to where he's laid,
The cattle trains go roaring down the one-in-thirty grade.
I wonder does he hear them pass and can he see the sight,
When through the dark the fast express goes flaming by at night?

'I think 'twould comfort him to know there's someone left to care,
I'll take some things this very night and hold a banquet there!
The hard old fare we've often shared together, him and me,
Some damper and a bite of beef, a pannikin of tea:
We'll do without the bands and flags, the speeches and the fuss,
We know who *ought* to get the cheers and that's enough for us.

'What's that? They wish that I'd come down—the oldest settler here!
Present me to the Governor and that young engineer!
Well, just you tell his Excellence and put the thing polite,
I'm sorry, but I can't come down—I'm dining out to-night!'

Bottle O!

I ain't the kind of bloke as takes to any steady job;
    I drives me bottle cart around the town;
A bloke what keeps 'is eyes about can always make a bob—
    I couldn't bear to graft for every brown.
There's lots of handy things about in everybody's yard,
    There's cocks and hens a-runnin' to an' fro,
And little dogs what comes and barks—we take 'em off their guard
    And we puts 'em with the Empty Bottle-O!

Chorus—

So it's any 'Empty bottles! Any empty bottle-O!'
    You can hear us round for half a mile or so.
And you'll see the women rushing
    To take in the Monday's washing
When they 'ear us crying, 'Empty Bottle-O!'

I'm drivin' down by Wexford-street and up a winder goes,
    A girl sticks out 'er 'ead and looks at me,
An all-right tart with ginger 'air, and freckles on 'er nose;
    I stops the cart and walks across to see.
'There ain't no bottles 'ere,' says she, 'since father took the pledge;'
    'No bottles 'ere,' says I, 'I'd like to know
What right you 'ave to stick your 'ead outside the winder ledge,
    If you 'aven't got no Empty Bottle-O!'

I sometimes gives the 'orse a spell, and then the push and me
    We takes a little trip to Chowder Bay.
Oh! ain't it nice the 'ole day long a-gazin' at the sea
    And a-hidin' of the tanglefoot away.
But when the booze gits 'old of us, and fellows starts to 'scrap',
    There's some what likes blue-metal for to throw:
But as for me, I always says for layin' out a 'trap'
    There's nothing like an Empty Bottle-O!

Father Riley's Horse

'Twas the horse thief, Andy Regan, that was hunted like a dog
    By the troopers of the upper Murray side,
They had searched in every gully—they had looked in every log,
    But never a sight or track of him they spied,
Till the priest at Kiley's Crossing heard a knocking very late
    And a whisper 'Father Riley—come across!'
So his Rev'rence in pyjamas trotted softly to the gate
    And admitted Andy Regan—and a horse!

'Now, it's listen, Father Riley, to the words I've got to say,
    For it's close upon my death I am tonight.
With the troopers hard behind me I've been hiding out all day
    In the gullies keeping close and out of sight.
But they're watching all the ranges till there's not a bird could fly,
    And I'm fairly worn to pieces with the strife,
So I'm taking no more trouble, but I'm going home to die,
    'Tis the only way I see to save my life.

'Yes, I'm making home to mother's and I'll die o' Tuesday next
An' be buried on the Thursday—and, of course,
I'm prepared to meet my penance, but with one thing I'm perplexed
And it's—Father, it's this jewel of a horse!
He was never bought nor paid for, and there's not a man can swear
To his owner or his breeder, but I know,
That his sire was by Pedantic from the Old Pretender mare
And his dam was close related to The Roe.

'And there's nothing in the district that can race him for a step,
He could canter while they're going at their top:
He's the king of all the leppers that was ever seen to lep,
A five-foot fence—he'd clear it in a hop!
So I'll leave him with you, Father, till the dead shall rise again,
'Tis yourself that knows a good 'un; and, of course,
You can say he's got by Moonlight out of Paddy Murphy's plain
If you're ever asked the breeding of the horse!

'But it's getting on to daylight and it's time to say goodbye,
For the stars above the east are growing pale.
And I'm making home to mother—and it's hard for me to die!
But it's harder still, is keeping out of gaol!
You can ride the old horse over to my grave across the dip
Where the wattle bloom is waving overhead.
Sure he'll jump them fences easy—you must never raise the whip
Or he'll rush 'em—now, goodbye!' and he had fled!

So they buried Andy Regan, and they buried him to rights,
In the graveyard at the back of Kiley's Hill;
There were five-and-twenty mourners who had five-and-twenty fights
Till the very boldest fighters had their fill.
There were fifty horses racing from the graveyard to the pub,
And the riders flogged each other all the while.
And the lashin's of the liquor! And the lavin's of the grub!
Oh, poor Andy went to rest in proper style.

Then the races came to Kiley's—with a steeplechase and all,
For the folk were mostly Irish round about,
And it takes an Irish rider to be fearless of a fall,
They were training morning in and morning out.
But they never started training till the sun was on the course
For superstitious story kept 'em back,
That the ghost of Andy Regan on a slashing chestnut horse,
Had been training by the starlight on the track.

And they read the nominations for the races with surprise
   And amusement at the Father's little joke,
For a novice had been entered for the steeplechasing prize,
   And they found that it was Father Riley's moke!
He was neat enough to gallop, he was strong enough to stay!
   But his owner's views of training were immense,
For the Reverend Father Riley used to ride him every day,
   And he never saw a hurdle nor a fence.

And the priest would join the laughter: 'Oh,' said he, 'I put him in,
   For there's five-and-twenty sovereigns to be won.
And the poor would find it useful, if the chestnut chanced to win,
   And he'll maybe win when all is said and done!'
He had called him Faugh-aballagh, which is French for 'clear the course',
   And his colours were a vivid shade of green:
All the Dooleys and O'Donnells were on Father Riley's horse,
   While the Orangemen were backing Mandarin!

It was Hogan, the dog poisoner—aged man and very wise,
   Who was camping in the racecourse with his swag,
And who ventured the opinion, to the township's great surprise,
   That the race would go to Father Riley's nag.
'You can talk about your riders—and the horse has not been schooled,
   And the fences is terrific, and the rest!
When the field is fairly going, then ye'll see ye've all been fooled,
   And the chestnut horse will battle with the best.

For there's some has got condition, and they think the race is sure,
   And the chestnut horse will fall beneath the weight,
But the hopes of all the helpless, and the prayers of all the poor,
   Will be running by his side to keep him straight.
And it's what's the need of schoolin' or of workin' on the track,
   Whin the saints are there to guide him round the course!
I've prayed him over every fence—I've prayed him out and back!
   And I'll bet my cash on Father Riley's horse!'

*   *   *

Oh, the steeple was a caution! They went tearin' round and round,
   And the fences rang and rattled where they struck.
There was some that cleared the water—there was more fell in and drowned,
   Some blamed the men and others blamed the luck!
But the whips were flying freely when the field came into view,
   For the finish down the long green stretch of course,

And in front of all the flyers—jumpin' like a kangaroo,
  Came the rank outsider—Father Riley's horse!

Oh, the shouting and the cheering as he rattled past the post!
  For he left the others standing, in the straight;
And the rider—well they reckoned it was Andy Regan's ghost,
  And it beat 'em how a ghost would draw the weight!
But he weighed in, nine stone seven, then he laughed and disappeared,
  Like a banshee (which is Spanish for an elf),
And old Hogan muttered sagely, 'If it wasn't for the beard
  They'd be thinking it was Andy Regan's self!'

And the poor of Kiley's Crossing drank the health at Christmastide
  Of the chestnut and his rider dressed in green.
There was never such a rider, not since Andy Regan died,
  And they wondered who on earth he could have been.
But they settled it among 'em, for the story got about,
  'Mongst the bushmen and the people on the course,
That the Devil had been ordered to let Andy Regan out
  For the steeplechase on Father Riley's horse!

The City of Dreadful Thirst

The stranger came from Narromine and made his little joke—
'They say we folks in Narromine are narrow-minded folk.
But all the smartest men down here are puzzled to define
A kind of new phenomenon that came to Narromine.

'Last summer up in Narromine 'twas gettin' rather warm—
Two hundred in the water-bag, and lookin' like a storm—
We all were in the private bar, the coolest place in town,
When out across the stretch of plain a cloud came rollin' down.

'We don't respect the clouds up there, they fill us with disgust,
They mostly bring a Bogan shower—three rain-drops and some dust;
But each man, simultaneous-like, to each man said "I think
That cloud suggests it's up to us to have another drink!"

'There's clouds of rain and clouds of dust—we'd heard of them before,
And sometimes in the daily press we read of "clouds of war":
But—if this ain't the Gospel truth I hope that I may burst—
That cloud that came to Narromine was just a cloud of thirst.

'It wasn't like a common cloud, 'twas more a sort of haze;
It settled down about the streets, and stopped for days and days,
And not a drop of dew could fall and not a sunbeam shine
To pierce that dismal sort of mist that hung on Narromine.

'Oh, Lord! we had a dreadful time beneath that cloud of thirst!
We all chucked-up our daily work and went upon the burst.
The very blacks about the town that used to cadge for grub,
They made an organised attack and tried to loot the pub.

'We couldn't leave the private bar no matter how we tried;
Shearers and squatters, union-men and blacklegs side by side
Were drinkin' there and dursn't move, for each was sure, he said,
Before he'd get a half-a-mile the thirst would strike him dead!

'We drank until the drink gave out, we searched from room to room,
And round the pub, like drunken ghosts, went howling through the gloom.
The shearers found some kerosene and settled down again,
But all the squatter chaps and I, we staggered to the train.

'And, once outside the cloud of thirst, we felt as right as pie,
But while we stopped about the town we had to drink or die.
But now I hear it's safe enough, I'm going back to work
Because they say the cloud of thirst has shifted on to Bourke.

'But when you see those clouds about—like this one over here—
All white and frothy at the top, just like a pint of beer,
It's time to go and have a drink, for if that cloud should burst
You'd find the drink would all be gone, for that's a cloud of thirst!'

We stood the man from Narromine a pint of half-and-half;
He drank it off without a gasp in one tremendous quaff; '
I joined some friends last night,' he said, 'in what *they* called a spree;
But after Narromine 'twas just a holiday to me.'

And now beyond the Western Range, where sunset skies are red,
And clouds of dust, and clouds of thirst, go drifting overhead,
The railway-train is taking back, along the Western Line,
That narrow-minded Person on his road to Narromine.

Santa Claus

'Halt! Who goes there?' The sentry's call
Rose on the midnight air
Above the noises of the camp,
The roll of wheels, the horses' tramp.
The challenge echoed over all—
'Halt! Who goes there?'

A quaint old figure clothed in white,
He bore a staff of pine,
An ivy-wreath was on his head.
'Advance, oh friend,' the sentry said,
'Advance, for this is Christmas night,
And give the countersign.'

'No sign nor countersign have I,
Through many lands I roam
The whole world over far and wide,
To exiles all at Christmastide,
From those who love them tenderly
I bring a thought of home.

'From English brook and Scottish burn,
From cold Canadian snows,
From those far lands ye hold most dear
I bring you all a greeting here,
A frond of a New Zealand fern,
A bloom of English rose.

'From faithful wife and loving lass
I bring a wish divine,
For Christmas blessings on your head.'
'I wish you well,' the sentry said,
'But here, alas! you may not pass
Without the countersign.'

He vanished—and the sentry's tramp
Re-echoed down the line.
It was not till the morning light
The soldiers knew that in the night
Old Santa Claus had come to camp
Without the countersign.

Driver Smith

'Twas Driver Smith of Battery A was anxious to see a fight;
He thought of the Transvaal all the day, he thought of it all the night—
'Well, if the battery's left behind, I'll go to the war,' says he,
'I'll go a-driving an ambulance in the ranks of the A.M.C.

'I'm fairly sick of these here parades, it's want of a change that kills
A-charging the Randwick Rifle Range and aiming at Surry Hills.
And I think if I go with the ambulance I'm certain to find a show,
For they have to send the Medical men wherever the troops can go.

'Wherever the rifle bullets flash and the Maxims raise a din,
It's there you'll find the Medical men a-raking the wounded in—
A-raking 'em in like human flies—and a driver smart like me
Will find some scope for his extra skill in the ranks of the A.M.C.'

So Driver Smith he went to the war a-cracking his driver's whip,
From ambulance to collecting base they showed him his regular trip.
And he said to the boys that were marching past, as he gave his whip a crack,
'You'll walk yourselves to the fight,' says he, 'Lord spare me, I'll drive you back.'

Now, the fight went on in the Transvaal hills for the half of a day or more,
And Driver Smith he worked his trip—all aboard for the seat of war!
He took his load from the stretcher men and hurried 'em homeward fast
Till he heard a sound that he knew full well—a battery rolling past.

He heard the clink of the leading chains and the roll of the guns behind—
He heard the crack of the drivers' whips, and he says to 'em, 'Strike me blind,
I'll miss me trip with this ambulance, although I don't care to shirk,
But I'll take the car off the line to-day and follow the guns at work.'

Then up the Battery Colonel came a-cursing 'em black in the face.
'Sit down and shift 'em, you drivers there, and gallop 'em into place.'
So off the Battery rolled and swung, a-going a merry dance,
And holding his own with the leading gun goes Smith with his ambulance.

They opened fire on the mountain side, a-peppering by and large,
When over the hill above their flank the Boers came down at the charge;
They rushed the guns with a daring rush, a-volleying left and right,
And Driver Smith with his ambulance moved up to the edge of the fight.

The gunners stuck to their guns like men, and fought like the wild cats fight,
For a Battery man don't leave his gun with ever a hope in sight;
But the bullets sang and the Mausers cracked and the Battery men gave way,
Till Driver Smith with his ambulance drove into the thick of the fray.

He saw the head of the Transvaal troop a-thundering to and fro,
A hard old face with a monkey beard—a face that he seemed to know;
'Now, who's that leader,' said Driver Smith, 'I've seen him before to-day.
Why, bless my heart, but it's Kruger's self,' and he jumped for him straight away.

He collared old Kruger round the waist and hustled him into the van.
It wasn't according to stretcher drill for raising a wounded man;
But he forced him in and said, 'All aboard, we're off for a little ride,
And you'll have the car to yourself,' says he, 'I reckon we're full inside.'

He wheeled his team on the mountain side and set 'em a merry pace,
A-galloping over the rocks and stones, and a lot of the Boers gave chase;
But Driver Smith had a fairish start, and he said to the Boers, 'Good-day,
You have Buckley's chance for to catch a man that was trained in Battery A.'

He drove his team to the hospital and said to the P.M.O.,
'Beg pardon, sir, but I missed a trip, mistaking the way to go;
And Kruger came to the ambulance and asked could we spare a bed,
So I fetched him here, and we'll take him home to show for a bob a head.'

So the word went round to the English troops to say they need fight no more,
For Driver Smith with his ambulance had ended the blooming war:
And in London now at the music halls he's starring it every night,
And drawing a hundred pounds a week to tell how he won the fight.

Right in the Front of the Army

'Where 'ave you been this week or more,
'Aven't seen you about the war?
Thought perhaps you was at the rear
Guarding the waggons.' 'What, us? No fear!
Where have we been? Why, bless my heart,
Where have we been since the bloomin' start?

'Right in the front of the army,
Battling day and night!
Right in the front of the army,
Teaching 'em how to fight!'
Every separate man you see,
Sapper, gunner, and C.I.V.,
Every one of 'em seems to be
Right in the front of the army!

Most of the troops to the camp had gone,
When we met with a cow-gun toiling on;
And we said to the boys, as they walked her past,
'Well, thank goodness, you're here at last!'
'Here at last! Why, what d'yer mean?
Ain't we just where we've always been?

'Right in the front of the army,
Battling day and night!
Right in the front of the army,
Teaching 'em how to fight!'
Correspondents and vets in force,
Mounted foot and dismounted horse,
All of them were, as a matter of course,
Right in the front of the army.

Old Lord Roberts will have to mind
If ever the enemy get behind;
For they'll smash him up with a rear attack,
Because his army has got no back!
Think of the horrors that might befall
An army without any rear at all!

Right in the front of the army,
Battling day and night!
Right in the front of the army,
Teaching 'em how to fight!
Swede attaches and German counts,
Yeomen (known as De Wet's remounts),
All of them were by their own accounts
Right in the front of the army!

The Scotch Engineer

With eyes that searched in the dark,
Peering along the line,
Stood the grim Scotchman, Hector Clark,
Driver of 'Forty-nine',
And the veldt-fire flamed on the hills ahead,
Like a blood-red beacon sign.

There was word of a fight to the north,
And a column hard-pressed,
So they started the Highlanders forth,
Without food, without rest.

But the pipers gaily played,
Chanting their fierce delight,
And the armoured carriages rocked and swayed,
Laden with men of the Scotch Brigade,
Hurrying up to the fight,
And the grim, grey Highland engineer,
Driving them into the night.

Then a signal light glowed red,
And a picket came to the track.
'Enemy holding the line ahead,
Three of our mates we have left for dead,
Only we two got back.'
And far to the north through the still night air,
They heard the rifles crack.

And the boom of a gun rang out,
Like the sound of a deep appeal,
And the picket stood in doubt
By the side of the driving-wheel.

But the Engineer looked down,
With his hand on the starting-bar,
'Ride ye back to the town,
Ye know what my orders are,
Maybe they're wanting the Scotch Brigade
Up on those hills afar.

'I am no soldier at all,
Only an engineer,
But I could not bear that the folk should say,
Over in Scotland—Glasgow way—
That Hector Clark stayed here
With the Scotch Brigade till the foe were gone,
With ever a rail to run her on.
Ready behind! Stand clear!

'Fireman, get you gone
Into the armoured train,
I will drive her alone;
One more trip—and perhaps the last—
With a well-raked fire and an open blast—
Hark to the rifles again.'

* * *

On through the choking dark,
Never a lamp nor a light,
Never an engine spark,
Showing her hurried flight.
Over the lonely plain
Rushed the great armoured-train,
Hurrying up to the fight.

Then with her living freight
On to the foe she came,
And the rifles snapped their hate,
And the darkness spouted flame.

Over the roar of the fray
The hungry bullets whined,
As she dashed through the foe that lay
Loading and firing blind,
Till the glare of the furnace burning clear
Showed them the form of the engineer,
Sharply and well defined.

Through! They were safely through!
Hark to the column's cheer!
Surely the driver knew
He was to halt her here;
But he took no heed of the signals red,
And the fireman found, when he climbed ahead,
There on the floor of his engine—dead,
Lay the Scotch Engineer!

Johnny Boer

Men fight all shapes and sizes as the racing horses run,
And no man knows his courage till he stands before a gun.
At mixed-up fighting, hand to hand, and clawing men about
They reckon Fuzzy-wuzzy is the hottest fighter out.
But Fuzzy gives himself away—his style is out of date,
He charges like a driven grouse that rushes on its fate;
You've nothing in the world to do but pump him full of lead:
But when you're fighting Johnny Boer you have to use your head;
He don't believe in front attacks or charging at the run,
He fights you from a kopje with his little Maxim gun.

For when the Lord He made the earth, it seems uncommon clear,
He gave the job of Africa to some good engineer,
Who started building fortresses on fashions of his own—
Lunettes, redoubts, and counterscarps all made of rock and stone.
The Boer needs only bring a gun, for ready to his hand
He finds these heaven-built fortresses all scattered through the land;
And there he sits and winks his eye and wheels his gun about,
And we must charge across the plain to hunt the beggar out.
It ain't a game that grows on us, there's lots of better fun
Than charging at old Johnny with his little Maxim gun.

On rocks a goat could scarcely climb, steep as the walls of Troy,
He wheels a four-point-seven about as easy as a toy;
With bullocks yoked and drag-ropes manned, he lifts her up the rocks
And shifts her every now and then, as cunning as a fox.
At night you mark her right ahead, you see her clean and clear,
Next day at dawn—'What, ho! she bumps'—from somewhere in the rear.
Or else the keenest-eyed patrol will miss him with the glass—
He's lying hidden in the rocks to let the leaders pass;
But when the main guard comes along he opens up the fun,
There's lots of ammunition for the little Maxim gun.

But after all the job is sure, although the job is slow,
We have to see the business through, the Boer has got to go.
With Nordenfeldt and lyddite shell it's certain, soon or late,
We'll hunt him from his kopjes and across the Orange State;
And then across those open flats you'll see the beggar run,
And we'll be running after with our little Maxim gun.

That V.C.

'Twas in the days of front attack,
  This glorious truth we'd yet to learn it—
That every 'front' had got a back,
  And French was just the man to turn it.

A wounded soldier on the ground
  Was lying hid behind a hummock;
He proved the good old proverb sound—
  An army travels on its stomach.

He lay as flat as any fish,
  His nose had worn a little furrow;
He only had one frantic wish,
  That like an antbear he could burrow.

The bullets whistled into space,
  The pom-pom gun kept up its braying,
The four-point-seven supplied the bass—
  You'd think the devil's band was playing.

A valiant comrade crawling near
  Observed his most supine behaviour,
And crept towards him, 'Hey! what cheer?
  Buck up,' said he, 'I've come to save yer.

'You get up on my shoulders, mate,
  And if we live beyond the firing,
I'll get the V.C. sure as fate,
  Because our blokes is all retiring.

'It's fifty pounds a year,' says he,
  'I'll stand you lots of beer and whisky.'
'No,' says the wounded man, 'not me,
  I'll not be saved, it's far too risky.

'I'm fairly safe behind this mound,
  I've worn a hole that seems to fit me;
But if you lift me off the ground,
  It's fifty pounds to one they'll hit me.'

So back towards the firing line
  Our friend crept slowly to the rear oh!
Remarking 'What a selfish swine!
  He might have let me be a hero.'

Jock!

There's a soldier that's been doing of his share
In the fighting up and down and round about.
He's continually marching here and there
And he's fighting, morning in and morning out.

The Boer, you see, he generally runs;
But sometimes when he hides behind a rock,
And we can't make no impression with the guns,
Oh, then you'll hear the order, 'Send for Jock!'

Yes, it's Jock—Scotch Jock.
He's the fellow that can give or take a knock.
For he's hairy and he's hard,
And his feet are by the yard,
And his face is like the face what's on a clock.
But when the bullets fly you will mostly hear the
cry—
'Send for Jock!'

The Cavalry have gun and sword and lance,
Before they choose their weapon, why, they're dead.
The Mounted Fut are hampered in advance
By holding of their helmets on their head.

And when the Boer has dug himself a trench
And placed his Maxim gun behind a rock,
These mounted heroes—pets of Johnny French—
They have to sit and wait and send for Jock!

Yes, the Jocks—Scotch Jocks,
With their music that'd terrify an ox!
When the bullets kick the sand
You can hear the sharp command—
'Forty-Second! At the double! Charge the rocks!'
And the charge is like a flood
When they've warmed the Highland blood
Of the Jocks!

The Last Parade

With never a sound of trumpet,
With never a flag displayed,
The last of the old campaigners
Lined up for the last parade.

Weary they were and battered,
Shoeless, and knocked about;
From under their ragged forelocks
Their hungry eyes looked out.

And they watched as the old commander
Read out, to the cheering men,
The Nation's thanks and the orders
To carry them home again.

And the last of the old campaigners,
Sinewy, lean, and spare—
He spoke for his hungry comrades:
'Have we not done our share?

'Starving and tired and thirsty
We limped on the blazing plain;
And after a long night's picket
You saddled us up again.

'We froze on the wind-swept kopjes
When the frost lay snowy-white.
Never a halt in the daytime,
Never a rest at night!

'We knew when the rifles rattled
From the hillside bare and brown,
And over our weary shoulders
We felt warm blood run down,

'As we turned for the stretching gallop,
Crushed to the earth with weight;
But we carried our riders through it—
Carried them p'raps too late.

'Steel! We were steel to stand it—
We that have lasted through,
We that are old campaigners
Pitiful, poor, and few.

'Over the sea you brought us,
Over the leagues of foam:
Now we have served you fairly
Will you not take us home?

'Home to the Hunter River,
To the flats where the lucerne grows;
Home where the Murrumbidgee
Runs white with the melted snows.

'This is a small thing surely!
Will not you give command
That the last of the old campaigners
Go back to their native land?'

They looked at the grim commander,
But never a sign he made.
'Dismiss!' and the old campaigners
Moved off from their last parade.

On the Trek

Oh, the weary, weary journey on the trek, day after day,
With sun above and silent veldt below;
And our hearts keep turning homeward to the youngsters far away,
And the homestead where the climbing roses grow.
Shall we see the flats grow golden with the ripening of the grain?
Shall we hear the parrots calling on the bough?
Ah! the weary months of marching ere we hear them call again,
For we're going on a long job now.

In the drowsy days on escort, riding slowly half asleep,
With the endless line of waggons stretching back,
While the khaki soldiers travel like a mob of travelling sheep,
Plodding silent on the never-ending track,
While the constant snap and sniping of the foe you never see
Makes you wonder will your turn come—when and how?
As the Mauser ball hums past you like a vicious kind of bee—
Oh! we're going on a long job now.

When the dash and the excitement and the novelty are dead,
And you've seen a load of wounded once or twice,
Or you've watched your old mate dying—with the vultures overhead,
Well, you wonder if the war is worth the price.
And down along Monaro now they're starting out to shear,
I can picture the excitement and the row;
But they'll miss me on the Lachlan when they call the roll this year,
For we're going on a long job now.

The Rum Parade

TUNE: 'BALLYHOOLEY'

Now ye gallant Sydney boys, who have left your household joys
To march across the sea in search of glory,
I am very much afraid that you do not love parade,
But the rum parade is quite another story.
For the influenza came and to spoil its little game,
They ordered we should drink a curious mixture;
Though at first it frightened some, when they found it mostly rum,
Parade became a very pleasant fixture.

Chorus

So it's forward the Brigade, if they'll hold a rum parade
At Pretoria there's nothing to alarm ye;
And it's easy to be seen if they'll leave out the quinine,
Ye'll be there before the blessed British Army.

Then a corporal he come and he said I drank the rum,
But the quinine never reached its destination;
For begob he up and swored that I threw it overboard,
Sure my heart was filled with grief and indignation.
For I'm different to some, I prefer quinine to rum,
And I only take the rum just as a favour,
And it's easy to be seen I'm so fond of the quinine,
That I keep it lest the rum should spoil its flavour.

When we get to Africay we'll be landed straight away,
And quartered with the troops of Queen Victoria;
And we hope they'll understand that the moment that we land
We are ready for a march upon Pretoria.
And we'll pay off all the scores on old Kruger and his Boers,
And just to prove our manners aren't a failure,
And to show we are not mean, shure we'll give them the quinine,
And drink the rum in honour of Australia.

What Have the Cavalry Done?

What have the cavalry done?
Cantered and trotted about,
Routin' the enemy out,
Causin' the beggars to run
And we tramped along the blazin' heat,
Over the veldt on our weary feet.
Tramp, tramp, tramp
Under the blazin' sun,
With never the sight of a bloomin' Boer,
'Cause they'd hunted 'em long before—
That's what the cavalry done!

What have the gunners done
Battlin' every day,
Battlin' any way.
Boers outranged 'em, but what cared they?
Shoot and be damned,' said the R.H.A.!
See! when the fight grows hot,
Under the rifles or not,
Always the order runs,
'Fetch up the bloomin' guns!'

And you'd see them great gun-horses spring
To the 'action front'—and around they'd swing.
Find the range with some queer machine
'At four thousand with fuse fourteen.
Ready! Fire number one!'
Handled the battery neat and quick!
Stick to it, too! How *did* they stick!
Never a gunner was seen to run!
Never a gunner would leave his gun!
Not though his mates dropped all around!
Always a gunner would stand his ground.
Take the army—the infantry,
Mounted rifles, and cavalry,
Twice the numbers I'd give away,
And I'd fight the lot with the R.H.A.,
For they showed us how a corps *should* be run,
That's what the gunners done!

There's Another Blessed Horse Fell Down

When you're lying in your hammock, sleeping soft and sleeping sound,
   Without a care or trouble on your mind,
And there's nothing to disturb you but the engines going round,
   And you're dreaming of the girl you left behind;
In the middle of your joys you'll be wakened by a noise,
   And a clatter on the deck above your crown,
And you'll hear the corporal shout as he turns the picket out,
   'There's another blessed horse fell down.'

You can see 'em in the morning, when you're cleaning out the stall,
   A-leaning on the railings nearly dead,

And you reckon by the evening they'll be pretty sure to fall,
  And you curse them as you tumble into bed.
Oh, you'll hear it pretty soon, 'Pass the word for Denny Moon,
  There's a horse here throwing handsprings like a clown;'
And it's 'Shove the others back or he'll cripple half the pack,
  There's another blessed horse fell down.'

And when the war is over and the fighting all is done,
  And you're all at home with medals on your chest,
And you've learnt to sleep so soundly that the firing of a gun
  At your bedside wouldn't rob you of your rest;
As you lie in slumber deep, if your wife walks in her sleep,
  And tumbles down the stairs and breaks her crown,
Oh, it won't awaken you, for you'll say, 'It's nothing new,
  It's another blessed horse fell down.'

Fed Up

I ain't a timid man at all, I'm just as brave as most,
I'll take my chance in open fight and die beside my post;
But riding round the 'ole day long as target for a Krupp,
A-drawing fire from Koppies well, I'm fair fed up.
It's wonderful how few get hit, it's luck that pulls us through;
Their rifle fire's no class at all, it misses me and you;
But when they sprinkle shells around like water from a cup
From that there blooming pom-pom gun—well, I'm fed up.

We never get a chance to charge, to do a thrust and cut,
I'll have to chuck the Cavalry and join the Mounted Fut.
But after all—What's Mounted Fut? I saw them t'other day,
They occupied a Koppie when the Boers had run away.
The Cavalry went riding on and seen a score of fights,
But there they kept them Mounted Fut three solid days and nights—
Three solid starving days and nights with scarce a bite or sup,
Well! after that on Mounted Fut I'm fair fed up.

And tramping with the Footies ain't as easy as it looks,
They scarcely ever see a Boer except in picture books.
They do a march of twenty mile that leaves 'em nearly dead,

And then they find the bloomin' Boers is twenty miles ahead.
Each Footy is as full of fight as any bulldog pup,
But walking forty miles to fight—well, I'm fed up!

So after all I think that when I leave the Cavalry
I'll either join the ambulance or else the A.S.C.;
They've always tucker in the plate and coffee in the cup,
But Bully Beef and Biscuits—well! I'm fair fed up!

A Singer of the Bush

There is waving of grass in the breeze
And a song in the air,
And a murmur of myriad bees
That toil everywhere.
There is scent in the blossom and bough,
And the breath of the Spring
Is as soft as a kiss on a brow—
And Spring-time I sing.

There is drought on the land, and the stock
Tumble down in their tracks
Or follow—a tottering flock—
The scrub-cutter's axe.
While ever a creature survives
The axes shall swing;
We are fighting with fate for their lives—
And the combat I sing.

Song of the Federation

As the nations sat together, grimly waiting—
The fierce old nations battle-scarred—
Grown grey in their lusting and their hating,
Ever armed and ever ready keeping guard,
Through the tumult of their warlike preparation
And the half-stilled clamour of the drums
Came a voice crying, 'Lo! a new-made nation,
To her place in the sisterhood she comes!'

And she came—she was beautiful as morning,
With the bloom of the roses in her mouth,
Like a young queen lavishly adorning
Her charms with the splendours of the South.

And the fierce old nations, looking on her,
Said, 'Nay, surely she were quickly overthrown,
Hath she strength for the burden laid upon her,
Hath she power to protect and guard her own?'

Then she spoke, and her voice was clear and ringing
In the ears of the nations old and grey,
Saying, 'Hark, and ye shall hear my children singing
Their war-song in countries far away.
They are strangers to the tumult of the battle,
They are few but their hearts are very strong,
'Twas but yesterday they called unto the cattle,
But they now sing Australia's marching song.'

Song of the Australians in Action

For the honour of Australia, our mother,
Side by side with our kin from over sea,
We have fought and we have tested one another,
And enrolled among the brotherhood are we.

There was never post of danger but we sought it
In the fighting, through the fire, and through the blood.
There was never prize so costly but we bought it,
Though we paid for its purchase with our blood.

Was there any road too rough for us to travel?
Was there any path too far for us to tread?
You can track us by the blood drops on the gravel
On the roads that we milestoned with our dead!

And for you, oh our young and anxious mother,
O'er your great gains keeping watch and ward,
Neither fearing nor despising any other,
We will hold your possessions with the sword.

Then they passed to the place of world-long sleeping,
The grey-clad figures with their dead,
To the sound of their women softly weeping
And the Dead March moaning at their head:
And the Nations, as the grim procession ended,
Whispered, 'Child! But ye have seen the price we pay,
From War may we ever be defended,
Kneel ye down, new-made Sister—Let us Pray!'

Song of the Pen

Not for the love of women toil we, we of the craft,
Not for the people's praise;
Only because our goddess made us her own and laughed,
Claiming us all our days.

Claiming our best endeavour—body and heart and brain
Given with no reserve—
Niggard is she towards us, granting us little gain;
Still, we are proud to serve.

Not unto us is given choice of the tasks we try,
Gathering grain or chaff;
One of her favoured servants toils at the epic high,
One, that a child may laugh.

Yet if we serve her truly in our appointed place,
Freely she doth accord
Unto her faithful servants always this saving grace,
Work is its own reward!

The Maori's Wool

Now, this is just a simple tale to tell the reader how
They civilized the Maori tribe at Rooti-iti-au.

The Maoris are a mighty race—the finest ever known;
Before the missionaries came they worshipped wood and stone;
They went to war and fought like fiends, and when the war was done
They pacified their conquered foes by eating every one.
But nowadays about the *pahs* in idleness they lurk,
Prepared to smoke or drink or talk—or anything but work.
The richest tribe in all the North in sheep and horse and cow
Were those who led their simple lives at Rooti-iti-au.

'Twas down to town at Wellington a noble Maori came,
A Rangatira of the best, Rerenga was his name—
(The word Rerenga means a 'snag'—but until he was gone
This didn't strike the folk he met—it struck them later on.)
He stalked into the Bank they call the 'Great Financial Hell',
And told the Chief Financial Fiend the tribe had wool to sell.
The Bold Bank Manager looked grave—the price of wool was high.
He said, 'We'll lend you what you need—we're not disposed to buy.

'You ship the wool to England, Chief !—You'll find it's good advice,
And meanwhile you can draw from us the local market price.'
The Chief he thanked him courteously and said he wished to state
In all the Rooti-iti tribe his *mana* would be great,
But still the tribe were simple folk, and did not understand
This strange finance that gave them cash without the wool in hand.
So off he started home again, with trouble on his brow,
To lay the case before the tribe at Rooti-iti-au.

They held a great *korero* in the Rooti-iti clan,
With speeches lasting half a day from every leading man.
They called themselves poetic names—'lost children in a wood';
They said the Great Bank Manager was *Kapai*—extra good !
And so they sent Rerenga down, full-powered and well-equipped,
To draw as much as he could get, and let the wool be shipped;
And wedged into a 'Cargo Tank', full up from stern to bow,
A mighty clip of wool went Home from Rooti-iti-au.

It was the Bold Bank Manager who drew a heavy cheque;
Rerenga cashed it thoughtfully, then clasped him round the neck;
A hug from him was not at all a thing you'd call a lark—
You see he lived on mutton-birds and dried remains of shark—

But still it showed his gratitude; and, as he pouched the pelf,
'I'll *haka* for you, sir,' he said, 'in honour of yourself!'
The *haka* is a striking dance—the sort they don't allow
In any place more civilized than Rooti-iti-au.

He *'haka'd'* most effectively—then, with an airy grace,
Rubbed noses with the Manager, and vanished into space.
But when the wool return came back, ah me, what sighs and groans!
For every bale of Maori wool was loaded up with stones!
Yes—thumping great New Zealand rocks among the wool they found;
On every rock the Bank had lent just eighteen-pence a pound.
And now the Bold Bank Manager, with trouble on his brow,
Is searching vainly for the chief from Rooti-iti-au.

The Protest

I say 'e *isn't* Remorse!
'Ow do I know?
Saw 'im on Riccarton course
Two year ago!
Think I'd forget any 'orse?
Course 'e's The Crow!

Bumper Maginnis and I
After a 'go',
Walkin' our 'orses to dry,
I says 'Hello!
What's that old black goin' by?'
Bumper says 'Oh!
That's an old cuddy of Flanagan's—
Runs as The Crow!'

Now they make out 'e's Remorse.
Well, but I *know.*
Soon as I came on the course
I says ' 'Ello!
'Ere's the old Crow.'

Once a man's seen any 'orse,
Course 'e must know.
Sure as there's wood in this table,
I say 'e's The Crow.

(Cross-examined by the Committee.J

Ow do I know the moke
After one sight?
S'posin' you met a bloke
Down town at night,
Wouldn't you know 'im again when you met 'im?
That's *'im* all right!

What was the brand on 'is 'ide?
I couldn't say,
Brands can be transmogrified.
That ain't the way—
It's the *look* of a 'orse and the way that 'e moves
That I'd know any day.

What was the boy on ’is back?
Why, ’e went past
All of a minute, and off down the track.
—‘The ’orse went as fast?’
True, so ’e did! But, my eyes, what a treat!
’Ow can I notice the ’ands and the seat
Of each bumble-faced kid of a boy that I meet?
Lor’! What a question to ast!

(Protest dismissed.)

The Wargeeilah Handicap

Wargeilah town is very small,
There’s no cathedral nor a club,
In fact the township, all in all,
Is just one unpretentious pub;
And there, from all the stations round,
The local sportsmen can be found.

The sportsmen of Wargeilah side
Are very few but very fit:
There’s scarcely any sport been tried
But what they held their own at it
In fact, to search their records o’er,
They held their own and something more.

’Twas round about Wargeilah town
An English new chum did infest:
He used to wander up and down
In baggy English breeches drest—
His mental aspect seemed to be
Just stolid self-sufficiency.

The local sportsmen vainly sought
His tranquil calm to counteract,
By urging that he should be brought
Within the Noxious Creatures Act.
‘Nay, harm him not,’ said one more wise,
‘He is a blessing in disguise!

‘You see, he wants to buy a horse
To ride, and hunt, and steeplechase,
And carry ladies, too, of course,
And pull a cart and win a race.
Good gracious! he must be a flat
To think he’ll get a horse like that!

‘But since he has so little sense
And such a lot of cash to burn
We’ll sell him some experience
By which alone a fool can learn.
Suppose we let him have The Trap
To win Wargeilah Handicap!’

And here, I must explain to you
That, round about Wargeilah run,
There lived a very aged screw
Whose days of brilliancy were done:
A grand old warrior in his prime—
But age will beat us all in time.

A trooper’s horse in seasons past
He did his share to keep the peace
But took to falling, and at last
Was cast for age from the Police.
A publican at Conroy’s Gap
Then bought and christened him The Trap.

When grass was good, and horses dear,
He changed his owner now and then
At prices ranging somewhere near
The neighbourhood of two pound ten:
And manfully he earned his keep
By yarding cows and ration sheep.

They brought him in from off the grass
And fed and groomed the old horse up;
His coat began to shine like glass—
You’d think he’d win the Melbourne Cup.
And when they’d got him fat and flash
They asked the new chum—fifty—cash!

And when he said the price was high,
Their indignation knew no bounds.
They said, 'It's seldom you can buy
A horse like that for fifty pounds!
We'll refund twenty if The Trap
Should fail to win the handicap

The deed was done, the price was paid,
The new chum put the horse in train:
The local sports were much afraid
That he would sad experience gain,
By racing with some shearer's hack,
Who'd beat him halfway round the track.

So, on this guileless English spark
They did most fervently impress
That he must keep the matter dark,
And not let any person guess
That he was purchasing The Trap
To win Wargeilah Handicap.

They spoke of 'spielers from the Bland,'
And 'champions from the Castlereagh',
And gave the youth to understand
That all of these would stop away,
And spoil the race, if they should hear
That they had got The Trap to fear.

'Keep dark! They'll muster thick as flies
When once the news gets sent around
We're giving such a splendid prize—
A Snowdon horse worth fifty pound!
They'll come right in from Dandaloo,
And find—that it's a gift to you!'

The race came on—with no display,
Nor any calling of the card,
But round about the pub all day
A crowd of shearers, drinking hard,
And using language in a strain
'Twere flattery to call profane.

Our hero, dressed in silk attire—
Blue jacket and a scarlet cap—
With boots that shone like flames of fire,
Now did his canter on The Trap,
And walked him up and round about,
Until the other steeds came out.

He eyed them with a haughty look,
But saw a sight that caught his breath!
It was! Ah John! The Chinee cook!
In boots and breeches! Pale as death!
Tied with a rope, like any sack,
Upon a piebald pony's back!

The next, a colt—all mud and burrs!
Half-broken, with a black boy up
Who said, 'You gim'me pair o' spurs,
I win the bloomin' Melbourne Cup!'
These two were to oppose
The Trap for the Wargeilah Handicap!

They're off! The colt whipped down his head,
And humped his back and gave a squeal,
And bucked into the drinking shed,
Revolving like a Cath'rine wheel!
Men ran like rats! The atmosphere
Was filled with oaths and pints of beer!

But up the course the bold Ah John
Beside The Trap raced neck and neck:
The boys had tied him firmly on,
Which ultimately proved his wreck,
The saddle turned, and, like a clown,
He rode some distance upside down.

His legs around the horse were tied,
His feet towards the heavens were spread,
He swung and bumped at every stride
And ploughed the ground up with his head!
And when they rescued him,
The Trap had won Wargeilah Handicap!

And no enquiries we could make
Could tell by what false statements swayed
Ah John was led to undertake
A task so foreign to his trade!
He only smiled and said,
'Hoo Ki! I stop topside, I win all 'li!'

But never, in Wargeilah Town,
Was heard so eloquent a cheer
As when the President came down,
And toasted, in Colonial Beer,
'The finest rider on the course!
The winner of the Snowdon Horse!'

'You go and get your prize,' he said,
'He's with a wild mob, somewhere round
The mountains near The Watershed;
He's honestly worth fifty pound,
A noble horse, indeed, to win,
But none of *us* can run him in!

'We've chased him poor, we've chased him fat,
We've run him till our horses dropped,
But by such obstacles as that
A man like you will not be stopped,
You'll go and yard him any day,
So here's your health! Hooray! Hooray!'

The day wound up with booze and blow
And fights till all were well content,
But of the new chum, all I know
Is shown by this advertisement—
'For Sale, the well-known racehorse Trap,
He won Wargeilah Handicap!'

Anthony Considine

Out in the wastes of the West countrie,
Out where the white stars shine,
Grim and silent as such men be,
Rideth a man with a history—
Anthony Considine.

For the ways of men they are manifold
As their differing views in life;
For some are sold for the lust of gold
And some for the lust of strife:
But this man counted the world well lost
For the love of his neighbour's wife.

They fled together, as those must flee
Whom all men hold in blame;
Each to the other must all things be
Who cross the gulf of iniquity
And live in the land of shame.

But a light-o'-love, if she sins with one,
She sinneth with ninety-nine:
The rule holds good since the world begun—
Since ever the streams began to run
And the stars began to shine.
The rule holds true, and he found it true—
Anthony Considine.

A nobler spirit had turned in scorn
From a love that was stained with mire;
A weaker being might mourn and mourn
For the loss of his Heart's Desire:
But the anger of Anthony Considine
Blazed up like a flaming fire.

And she, with her new love, presently
Came past with her eyes ashine;
And God so willed it, and God knows why,
She turned and laughed as they passed him by—
Anthony Considine.

Her laughter stung as a whip might sting;
And mad with his wounded pride
He turned and sprang with a panther's spring
And struck at his rival's side:
And only the woman, shuddering,
Could tell how the dead man died!

She dared not speak—and the mystery
Is buried in auld lang syne,
But out on the wastes of the West countrie,
Grim and silent as such men be,
Rideth a man with a history—
Anthony Considine.

The Angel's Kiss

An angel stood beside the bed
Where lay the living and the dead.

He gave the mother—her who died—
A kiss that Christ the Crucified

Had sent to greet the weary soul
When, worn and faint, it reached its goal.

He gave the infant kisses twain,
One on the breast, one on the brain.

'Go forth into the world,' he said,
'With blessings on your heart and head,

'For God, who ruleth righteously,
Hath ordered that to such as be

'From birth deprived of mother's love,
I bring His blessing from above;

'But if the mother's life he spare
Then she is made God's messenger

'To kiss and pray that heart and brain
May go through life without a stain.'

The infant moved towards the light,
The angel spread his wings in flight.

But each man carries to his grave
The kisses that in hopes to save
The angel or his mother gave.

Any Other Time

All of us play our very best game—
  Any other time.
Golf or billiards, it's all the same—
  Any other time.
Lose a match and you always say,
'Just my luck! I was "off" to-day!
I could have beaten him quite half-way—
  Any other time!'

After a fiver you ought to go—
  Any other time.
Every man you ask says 'Oh,
  Any *other* time.
Lend you a fiver! I'd lend you two,
But I'm overdrawn and my bills are due,
Wish you'd ask me—now, mind you do—
  Any other time!'

Fellows will ask you out to dine—
  Any other time.
'Not to-night, for we're twenty-nine—
  Any other time.
Not to-morrow, for cook's on strike,
Not next day, I'll be out on the bike—
Just drop in whenever you like—
  Any other time!'
Seasick passengers like the sea—
  Any other time.

'Something . . I ate . . disagreed . . with me!
  Any other time
Ocean-trav'lling is . . simply bliss,
Must be my . . liver . . has gone amiss . .
Why, I would . . laugh . . at a sea . . like this—
  Any other time.'

Most of us mean to be better men—
  Any other time:
Regular upright characters then—
  Any other time.
Yet somehow as the years go by
Still we gamble and drink and lie,
When it comes to the last we'll want to die
  Any other time!

At the Melting of the Snow

There's a sunny Southern land,
  And it's there that I would be
Where the big hills stand,
  In the South Countrie!
When the wattles bloom again,
  Then it's time for us to go
To the old Monaro country
  At the melting of the snow.

To the East or to the West,
  Or wherever you may be,
You will find no place
  Like the South Countrie.
For the skies are blue above,
  And the grass is green below,
In the old Monaro country
  At the melting of the snow.

Now the team is in the plough,
  And the thrushes start to sing,
And the pigeons on the bough
  Are rejoicing at the Spring.
So come my comrades all,
  Let us saddle up and go
To the old Monaro country
  At the melting of the snow.

Barney Devine

TUNE: 'PADDY MCGHEE'

Where are you roving now, Barney Devine,
Shearing or droving now, what is your line?
Oh, but it's years since the last that we heard,
Never a mailman has brought us a word.
Chorus
Anyhow, anywhere, country or town,
Making the money or knocking it down.
Drought or wet weather, in rain or in shine,
Here's a long life to you, Barney Devine!

Say, are you shearing away in the west,
You that were always the fastest and best,
Shearing a hundred with never a scratch!
Where was the shearer could turn out their match?

Out on the cattle camps waiting for light,
Watching the stock in the hush of the night,
Singing your songs of the bush and its ways,
Telling your tales of the wandering days.

Far, far away though you happen to roam,
Ne'er you'll forget them the old folks at home,
Sadly they wait for a word or a line
Won't you come back to them, Barney Devine?

General Drought and General Rain

Parched are the plains and bare,
Dusty and eaten out:
Animals everywhere
Perish in dumb despair;
For the land is held in the iron grip
Of the enemy General Drought!

Who shall deliver us?
Who shall assuage our pain?
Men in their bitter grief,
Pray that they get relief,
That help may come from the friendly hand
Of our ally, General Rain.

Look at those flying mists
Sweeping across the plain!
These are the lads of the Light Brigade,
Light but fearless and undismayed;
They are the van of the first attack
Of the valiant General Rain.

Now are the Light Brigade
Baffled and beaten back:
But the blast of the rain-wind fifing clear,
Rallies its forces far and near
On to the grand attack.

Out of the stormy south
To the sound of the thunder's drum,
Peal upon peal, and crash on crash,
To the heliograph of the lightning flash,
The big battalions come!

Look at those big black clouds,
Gathering out at sea!
Never the swiftest war horse yet
Moved as they move, all stern and set,
On to their victory!

Never a Maxim Gun
Shoots like the stinging hail,

Never the blast of a fifer rings
Clear as the call that the storm wind sings
As the foe begins to fail.

Now may our thanks ascend
Over the smiling plain.
Thanks let us give that the foe falls back,
Crushed by the might of the fierce attack
Of the valiant General Rain.

The Gundaroo Bullock

Oh, there's some that breeds the Devon that's as solid as a stone,
And there's some that breeds the brindle which they call the 'Goulburn Roan';
But amongst the breeds of cattle there are very, very few
Like the hairy-whiskered bullock that they bred at Gundaroo.

Far away by Grabben Gullen, where the Murrumbidgee flows,
There's a block of broken countryside where no one ever goes;
For the banks have gripped the squatters, and the free selectors too,
And their stock are always stolen by the men of Gundaroo.

There came a low informer to the Grabben Gullen side,
And he said to Smith the squatter, 'You must saddle up and ride,
For your bullock's in the harness-cask of Morgan Donahoo—
He's the greatest cattle-stealer that abides in Gundaroo.'

'Oh, ho!' said Smith, the owner of the Grabben Gullen run,
'I'll go and get the troopers by the sinking of the sun,
And down into his homestead tonight we'll take a ride,
With warrants to identify the carcase and the hide.'

That night rode down the troopers, the squatter at their head,
They rode into the homestead, and pulled Morgan out of bed.
'Now, show to us the carcase of the bullock that you slew—
The great marsupial bullock that you killed in Gundaroo.'

They peered into the harness-cask, and found it wasn't full,
But down among the brine they saw some flesh and bits of wool.
'What's this?' exclaimed the trooper—'an infant, I declare,'
Said Morgan, ' 'Tis the carcase of an old man native bear.
I heard that ye were coming, so an old man bear I slew,
Just to give you kindly welcome to my home in Gundaroo.

'The times is something awful, as you can plainly see,
The banks have broke the squatters, and they've broke the likes of me;
We can't afford a bullock—such expense would never do—
So an old man bear for breakfast is a treat in Gundaroo.'

And along by Grabben Gullen where the rushing river flows,
In the block of broken country where there's no one ever goes,
On the Upper Murrumbidgee they're a hospitable crew,
But you mustn't ask for 'bullock' when you go to Gundaroo.

Hard Luck

I left the course, and by my side
  There walked a ruined tout—
A hungry creature evil-eyed,
  Who poured this story out.

'You see,' he said, 'there came a swell
  To Kensington to-day,
And if I picked the winners well,
  A crown at least he'd pay.

'I picked three winners straight, I did,
  I filled his purse with pelf,
And then he gave me half-a-quid,
  To back one for myself.

'A half-a-quid to me he cast,
  I wanted it indeed
So help me Bob, for two days past
  I haven't had a feed.

'But still I thought my luck was in,
  I couldn't go astray,
I put it all on Little Min,
  And lost it straightaway.

'I haven't got a bite or bed,
  I'm absolutely stuck,
So keep this lesson in your head:
  Don't over-trust your luck!'

The folks went homeward, near and far,
  The tout, Oh! where was he?
Ask where the empty boilers are,
  Beside the Circular Quay.

He Giveth His Beloved Sleep

The long day passes with its load of sorrow:
In slumber deep
I lay me down to rest until to-morrow—
Thank God for sleep.

Thank God for all respite from weary toiling,
From cares that creep
Across our lives like evil shadows, spoiling
God's kindly sleep.

We plough and sow, and, as the hours grow later,
We strive to reap,
And build our barns, and hope to build them greater
Before we sleep.

We toil and strain and strive with one another
In hopes to heap
Some greater share of profit than our brother
Before we sleep.

What will it profit that with tears or laughter
Our watch we keep?
Beyond it all there lies the Great Hereafter !
Thank God for sleep !

For, at the last, beseeching Christ to save us,
We turn with deep
Heart-felt thanksgiving unto God, who gave us
The Gift of Sleep.

In the Stable

What! You don't like him, well, maybe—we all have our fancies, of course:
Brumby to look at you reckon? Well, no: he's a thoroughbred horse;
Sired by a son of old Panic—look at his ears and his head—
Lop-eared and Roman-nosed, ain't he?—well, that's how the Panics are bred.
Gluttonous, ugly and lazy, rough as a tip-cart to ride,
Yet if you offered a sovereign apiece for the hairs on his hide
That wouldn't buy him, nor twice that; while I've a pound to the good,
This here old stager stays by me and lives like a thoroughbred should;
Hunt him away from his bedding, and sit yourself down by the wall,
Till you hear how the old fellow saved me from Gilbert, O'Meally and Hall.

* * *

Gilbert and Hall and O'Meally, back in the bushranging days,
Made themselves kings of the district—ruled it in old-fashioned ways—
Robbing the coach and the escort, stealing our horses at night,
Calling sometimes at the homesteads and giving the women a fright:
Came to the station one morning—and why they did this no one knows—
Took a brood mare from the paddock—wanting some fun, I suppose—
Fastened a bucket beneath her, hung by a strap round her flank,
Then turned her loose in the timber back of the seven-mile tank.

Go! She went mad! She went tearing and screaming with fear through the trees,
While the curst bucket beneath her was banging her flanks and her knees.

Bucking and racing and screaming she ran to the back of the run,
Killed herself there in a gully; by God, but they paid for their fun!
Paid for it dear, for the black-boys found tracks, and the bucket, and all,
And I swore that I'd live to get even with Gilbert, O'Meally and Hall.

Day after day then I chased them—'course they had friends on the sly,
Friends who were willing to sell them to those who were willing to buy.
Early one morning we found them in camp at the Cockatoo Farm
One of us shot at O'Meally and wounded him under the arm:
Ran them for miles in the ranges, till Hall, with his horse fairly beat,
Took to the rocks and we lost him—the others made good their retreat.
It was war to the knife then, I tell you, and once, on the door of my shed,
They nailed up a notice that offered a hundred reward for my head!

Then we heard they were gone from the district they stuck up a coach in the West,
And I rode by myself in the paddocks, taking a bit of a rest,
Riding this colt as a youngster—awkward, half-broken and shy,
He wheeled round one day on a sudden; I looked, but I couldn't see why,
But I soon found out why, for before me, the hillside rose up like a wall,
And there on the top with their rifles were Gilbert, O'Meally and Hall!

'Twas a good three-mile run to the homestead—bad going, with plenty of trees—
So I gathered the youngster together, and gripped at his ribs with my knees.
'Twas a mighty poor chance to escape them! It puts a man's nerve to the test
On a half-broken colt to be hunted by the best mounted men in the West.
But the half-broken colt was a racehorse! He lay down to work with a will,
Flashed through the scrub like a clean-skin—by Heavens we *flew* down the hill!
Over a twenty-foot gully he swept with the spring of a deer
And they fired as we jumped, but they missed me—a bullet sang close to my ear
And the jump gained us ground, for they shirked it: but I saw as we raced through the gap
That the rails at the homestead were fastened—I was caught like a rat in a trap.
Fenced with barbed wire was the paddock—barbed wire that would cut like a knife—
How was a youngster to clear it that never had jumped in his life?

Bang went a rifle behind me—the colt gave a spring, he was hit;
Straight at the sliprails I rode him—I felt him take hold of the bit;
Never a foot to the right or the left did he swerve in his stride,
Awkward and frightened, but honest, the sort it's a pleasure to ride!
Straight at the rails, where they'd fastened barbed wire on the top of the post,
Rose like a stag and went over, with hardly a scratch at the most;
Into the homestead I darted, and snatched down my gun from the wall,
And I tell you I made them step lively, Gilbert, O'Meally and Hall!

Yes! There's the mark of the bullet—he's got it inside of him yet
Mixed up somehow with his victuals, but bless you he don't seem to fret!

Gluttonous, ugly, and lazy—eats any thing he can bite;
Now let us shut up the stable, and bid the old fellow good-night:

Ah! We can't breed 'em, the sort that were bred when we old 'uns were young. . .
Yes, I was saying, these bushrangers, none of 'em lived to be hung,
Gilbert was shot by the troopers, Hall was betrayed by his friend,
Campbell disposed of O'Meally, bringing the lot to an end.
But you can talk about riding—I've ridden a lot in the past—
Wait till there's rifles behind you, you'll know what it means to go fast!
I've steeplechased, raced, and 'run horses', but I think the most dashing of all
Was the ride when the old fellow saved me from Gilbert, O'Meally and Hall!

The Last Trump

'You led the trump,' the old man said
With fury in his eye,
'And yet you hope my girl to wed!
Young man! your hopes of love are fled,
'Twere better she should die!

'My sweet young daughter sitting there,
So innocent and plump!
You don't suppose that she would care
To wed an outlawed man who'd dare
To lead the thirteenth trump!

'If you had drawn their leading spade
It meant a certain win!
But no! By Pembroke's mighty shade
The thirteenth trump you went and played
And let their diamonds in!

'My girl! Return at my command
His presents in a lump!
Return his ring! For understand
No man is fit to hold your hand
Who leads a thirteenth trump!

'But hold! Give every man his due
And every dog his day.
Speak up and say what made you do
This dreadful thing—that is, if you
Have anything to say!'

He spoke. 'I meant at first,' said he,
'To give their spades a bump:
Or lead the hearts, but then you see
I thought against us there might be,
Perhaps, a fourteenth trump!'

They buried him at dawn of day
Beside a ruined stump:
And there he sleeps the hours away
And waits for Gabriel to play
The last—the fourteenth—trump.

Not On It

The new chum's polo pony was the smartest pony yet—
The owner backed it for the Cup for all that he could get.
The books were laying fives to one, in tenners; and you bet
He was on it.

The bell was rung, the nags came out their quality to try,
The band played, "What Ho! Robbo!" as our hero cantered by,
The people in the Leger Stand cried out, "Hi, mister, hi!
Are you on it?"

They watched him as the flag went down; his fate is quickly told—
The pony gave a sudden spring, and off the rider rolled.
The pony finished first all right, but then our hero bold
Was not on it.

The Old Australian Ways

The London lights are far abeam
Behind a bank of cloud,
Along the shore the gas lights gleam,
The gale is piping loud;
And down the Channel, groping blind,
We drive her through the haze
Towards the land we left behind—
The good old land of 'never mind',
And old Australian ways.

The narrow ways of English folk
Are not for such as we;
They bear the long-accustomed yoke
Of staid conservancy:
But all our roads are new and strange
And through our blood there runs
The vagabonding love of change
That drove us westward of the range
And westward of the suns.

The city folk go to and fro
Behind a prison's bars,
They never feel the breezes blow
And never see the stars;
They never hear in blossomed trees
The music low and sweet
Of wild birds making melodies,
Nor catch the little laughing breeze
That whispers in the wheat.

Our fathers came of roving stock
That could not fixed abide:
And we have followed field and flock
Since e'er we learnt to ride;
By miner's camp and shearing shed,
In land of heat and drought,
We followed where our fortunes led,
With fortune always on ahead
And always further out.

The wind is in the barley grass,
The wattles are in bloom;
The breezes greet us as they pass
With honey-sweet perfume;
The parakeets go screaming by
With flash of golden wing,
And from the swamp the wild ducks cry
Their long-drawn note of revelry,
Rejoicing at the spring.

So throw the weary pen aside
And let the papers rest,
For we must saddle up and ride
Towards the blue hill's breast;
And we must travel far and fast
Across their rugged maze,
To find the Spring of Youth at last,
And call back from the buried past
The old Australian ways.

When Clancy took the drover's track
In years of long ago,
He drifted to the outer back
Beyond the Overflow;

By rolling plain and rocky shelf,
With stockwhip in his hand,
He reached at last, oh lucky elf,
The Town of Come-and-Help-Yourself
In Rough-and-Ready Land.

And if it be that you would know
The tracks he used to ride,
Then you must saddle up and go
Beyond the Queensland side—
Beyond the reach of rule or law,
To ride the long day through,
In Nature's homestead—filled with awe:
You then might see what Clancy saw
And know what Clancy knew.

The Old Timer's Steeplechase

The sheep were shorn and the wool went down
At the time of our local racing:
And I'd earned a spell—I was burnt and brown—
So I rolled my swag for a trip to town
And a look at the steeplechasing.

'Twas rough and ready—an uncleared course
As rough as the blacks had found it;
With barbed-wire fences, topped with gorse,
And a water-jump that would drown a horse,
And the steeple three times round it.

There was never a fence the tracks to guard—
Some straggling posts defined 'em:
And the day was hot, and the drinking hard,
Till none of the stewards could see a yard
Before nor yet behind 'em!

But the bell was rung and the nags were out,
Excepting an old outsider
Whose trainer started an awful rout,
For his boy had gone on a drinking bout
And left him without a rider.

'Is there not one man in the crowd,' he cried,
'In the whole of the crowd so clever,
Is there not one man that will take a ride
On the old white horse from the Northern side
That was bred on the Mooki River?'

'Twas an old white horse that they called The Cow,
And a cow would look well beside him;
But I was pluckier then than now
(And I wanted excitement anyhow),
So at last I agreed to ride him.

And the trainer said, 'Well, he's dreadful slow,
And he hasn't a chance whatever;
But I'm stony broke, so it's time to show
A trick or two that the trainers know
Who train by the Mooki River.

'The first time round at the further side,
With the trees and the scrub about you,
Just pull behind them and run out wide
And then dodge into the scrub and hide,
And let them go round without you.

'At the third time round, for the final spin
With the pace, and the dust to blind 'em,
They'll never notice if you chip in
For the last half-mile you'll be sure to win,
And they'll think you raced behind 'em.

'At the water-jump you may have to swim—
He hasn't a hope to clear it—
Unless he skims like the swallows skim
At full speed over, but not for him!
He'll never go next or near it.

'But don't you worry—just plunge across,
For he swims like a well-trained setter.
Then hide away in the scrub and gorse
The rest will be far ahead of course—
The further ahead the better.

'You must rush the jumps in the last half-round
For fear that he might refuse 'em;
He'll try to baulk with you, I'll be bound,
Take whip and spurs on the mean old hound,
And don't be afraid to use 'em.

'At the final round, when the field are slow
And you are quite fresh to meet 'em,
Sit down, and hustle him all you know
With the whip and spurs, and he'll have to go—
Remember, you've got to beat 'em!'

The flag went down and we seemed to fly,
And we made the timbers shiver
Of the first big fence, as the stand flashed by,
And I caught the ring of the trainer's cry:
'Go on! For the Mooki River!'

I jammed him in with a well-packed crush,
And recklessly—out for slaughter—
Like a living wave over fence and brush
We swept and swung with a flying rush,
Till we came to the dreaded water.

Ha, ha! I laugh at it now to think
Of the way I contrived to work it.
Shut in amongst them, before you'd wink,
He found himself on the water's brink,
With never a chance to shirk it!

The thought of the horror he felt, beguiles
The heart of this grizzled rover!
He gave a snort you could hear for miles,
And a spring would have cleared the Channel Isles
And carried me safely over!

Then we neared the scrub, and I pulled him back
In the shade where the gum-leaves quiver:
And I waited there in the shadows black
While the rest of the horses, round the track,
Went on like a rushing river!

At the second round, as the field swept by,
I saw that the pace was telling;
But on they thundered, and by-and-by
As they passed the stand I could hear the cry
Of the folk in the distance, yelling!

Then the last time round! And the hoofbeats rang!
And I said, 'Well, it's now or never!'
And out on the heels of the throng I sprang,
And the spurs bit deep and the whipcord sang
As I rode! For the Mooki River!

We raced for home in a cloud of dust
And the curses rose in chorus.
'Twas flog, and hustle, and jump you must!
And The Cow ran well—but to my disgust
There was one got home before us.

'Twas a big black horse, that I had not seen
In the part of the race I'd ridden;
And his coat was cool and his rider clean,
And I thought that perhaps I had not been
The only one that had hidden.

And the trainer came with a visage blue
With rage, when the race concluded:
Said he, 'I thought you'd have pulled us through,
But the man on the black horse planted too,
And nearer to home than you did!'

Alas to think that those times so gay
Have vanished and passed for ever!
You don't believe in the yarn you say?
Why, man! 'Twas a matter of every day
When we raced on the Mooki River!

The Passing of 'Gundagai'

'I'll introdooce a friend!' he said,
'And if you've got a vacant pen
You'd better take him in the shed
And start him shearing straight ahead,
He's one of these here quiet men.

'He never strikes—that ain't his game;
No matter what the others try
He goes on shearing just the same.
I never rightly knew his name—
We always call him "Gundagai"!'

Our flashest shearer then had gone
To train a racehorse for a race,
And while his sporting fit was on
He couldn't be relied upon,
So 'Gundagai' shore in his place.

Alas for man's veracity!
For reputations false and true!
This 'Gundagai' turned out to be,
For strife and all-round villainy,
The very worst I ever knew!

He started racing Jack Devine,
And grumbled when I made him stop.
The pace he showed was extra fine,
But all those pure-bred ewes of mine
Were bleeding like a butcher's shop.

He cursed the sheep, he cursed the shed,
From roof to rafter, floor to shelf;
As for my mongrel ewes, he said,
I ought to get a razor blade
And shave the blooming things myself.

On Sundays he controlled a 'school',
And played 'two-up' the livelong day;
And many a young confiding fool
He shore of his financial wool;
And when he lost he would not pay.

He organised a shearers' race,
And 'touched' me to provide the prize.
His packhorse showed surprising pace
And won hands down—he was The Ace,
A well-known racehorse in disguise.

Next day the bruiser of the shed
Displayed an opal-tinted eye,
With large contusions on his head.
He smiled a sickly smile, and said
He'd 'had a cut at "Gundagai"!'

But just as we were getting full
Of 'Gundagai' and all his ways,
A telegram for 'Henry Bull'
Arrived. Said he, 'That's me—all wool!
Let's see what this here message says.'

He opened it, his face grew white,
He dropped the shears and turned away.
It ran, 'Your wife took bad last night;
Come home at once—no time to write,
We fear she may not last the day.'

He got his cheque—I didn't care
To dock him for my mangled ewes;
His store account—we 'called it square'.
Poor wretch! he had enough to bear,
Confronted by such dreadful news.

The shearers raised a little purse
To help a mate, as shearers will,
'To pay the doctor and the nurse,
And if there should be something worse—
To pay the undertaker's bill.'

They wrung his hand in sympathy,
He rode away without a word,
His head hung down in misery...
A wandering hawker passing by
Was told of what had just occurred.

'Well! that's a curious thing,' he said,
'I've known that feller all his life—
He's had the loan of this here shed!
I know his wife ain't nearly dead,
Because he *hasn't got a wife!*'

You should have heard the whipcord crack
As angry shearers galloped by,
In vain they tried to fetch him back.
A little dust along the track
Was all they saw of 'Gundagai'.

The Pearl Diver

Kanzo Makame, the diver, sturdy and small Japanee,
Seeker of pearls and of pearl-shell down in the depths of the sea,
Trudged o'er the bed of the ocean, searching industriously.

Over the pearl-grounds, the lugger drifted—a little white speck:
Joe Nagasaki, the 'tender', holding the life-line on deck,
Talked through the rope to the diver, knew when to drift or to check.

Kanzo was king of his lugger, master and diver in one,
Diving wherever it pleased him, taking instructions from none;
Hither and thither he wandered, steering by stars and by sun.

Fearless he was beyond credence, looking at death eye to eye:
This was his formula always, 'All man go dead by-and-by—
'S'posing time come no can help it—s'pose time no come, then no die.'

Dived in the depths of the Darnleys, down twenty fathom and five;
Down where by law and by reason, men are forbidden to dive;
Down in a pressure so awful that only the strongest survive:

Sweated four men at the air pumps, fast as the handles could go,
Forcing the air down that reached him heated, and tainted, and slow—
Kanzo Makame the diver stayed seven minutes below;

Came up on deck like a dead man, paralysed body and brain;
Suffered, while blood was returning, infinite tortures of pain:
Sailed once again to the Darnleys—laughed and descended again!

* * *

Scarce grew the shell in the shallows, rarely a patch could they touch;
Always the take was so little, always the labour so much;
Always they thought of the Islands held by the lumbering Dutch,

Islands where shell was in plenty lying in passage and bay,
Islands where divers could gather hundreds of shell in a day:
But the lumbering Dutch, with their gunboats, hunted the divers away.

Joe Nagasaki, the 'tender', finding the profits grow small,
Said, 'Let us go to the Islands, try for a number one haul!
If we get caught, go to prison—let them take lugger and all!'

Kanzo Makame, the diver—knowing full well what it meant—
Fatalist, gambler, and stoic, smiled a broad smile of content,
Flattened in mainsail and foresail, and off to the Islands they went.

Close to the headlands they drifted, picking up shell by the ton,
Piled up on deck were the oysters, opening wide in the sun,
When, from the lee of the headland, boomed the report of a gun.

Once that the diver was sighted, pearl-shell and lugger must go.
Joe Nagasaki decided—quick was the word and the blow—
Cut both the pipe and the life-line, leaving the diver below!

Kanzo Makame, the diver, failing to quite understand,
Pulled the 'haul up' on the life-line, found it was slack in his hand;
Then, like a little brown stoic, lay down and died on the sand.

Joe Nagasaki, the 'tender', smiling a sanctified smile,
Headed her straight for the gunboat—throwing out shells all the while—
Then went aboard and reported, 'No makee dive in three mile!

'Dress no have got and no helmet—diver go shore on the spree;
Plenty wind come and break rudder—lugger get blown out to sea:
Take me to Japanese Consul, he help a poor Japanee!'

So the Dutch let him go, and they watched him, as off from the Islands he ran,
Doubting him much, but what would you? You have to be sure of your man
Ere you wake up that nestful of hornets—the little brown men of Japan.

Down in the ooze and the coral, down where earth's wonders are spread,
Helmeted, ghastly, and swollen, Kanzo Makame lies dead:
Joe Nagasaki, his 'tender', is owner and diver instead.

Wearer of pearls in your necklace, comfort yourself if you can,
These are the risks of the pearling—these are the ways of Japan,
'Plenty more Japanese diver, plenty more little brown man!'

Road to Gundagai

The mountain road goes up and down,
From Gundagai to Tumut town.

And branching off there runs a track,
Across the foothills grim and black,

Across the plains and ranges grey
To Sydney city far away.

It came by chance one day that I
From Tumut rode to Gundagai.

And reached about the evening tide
The crossing where the roads divide;

And, waiting at the crossing place,
I saw a maiden fair of face,

With eyes of deepest violet blue,
And cheeks to match the rose in hue—

The fairest maids Australia knows
Are bred among the mountain snows.

Then, fearing I might go astray,
I asked if she could show the way.

Her voice might well a man bewitch—
Its tones so supple, deep, and rich.

'The tracks are clear,' she made reply,
'And this goes down to Sydney town,
And that one goes to Gundagai.'

Then slowly, looking coyly back,
She went along the Sydney track.

And I for one was well content
To go the road the lady went;

But round the turn a swain she met—
The kiss she gave him haunts me yet!

I turned and travelled with a sigh
The lonely road to Gundagai.

The Road to Old Man's Town

The fields of youth are filled with flowers,
The wine of youth is strong:
What need have we to count the hours?
The summer days are long.

But soon we find to our dismay
That we are drifting down
The barren slopes that fall away
Towards the foothills grim and grey
That lead to Old Man's Town.

And marching with us on the track
Full many friends we find:
We see them looking sadly back
For those that dropped behind.

But God forbid a fate so dread—
Alone to travel down
The dreary road we all must tread,
With faltering steps and whitening head,
The road to Old Man's Town !

It's Grand

It's grand to be a squatter
  And sit upon a post,
And watch your little ewes and lambs
  A-giving up the ghost.

It's grand to be a 'cockie'
  With wife and kids to keep,
And find an all-wise Providence
  Has mustered all your sheep.

It's grand to be a western man,
  With shovel in your hand,
To dig your little homestead out
  From underneath the sand.

It's grand to be a shearer,
  Along the Darling side,
And pluck the wool from stinking sheep
  That some days since have died.

It's grand to be a rabbit
  And breed to all is blue,
And then to die in heaps because
  There's nothing left to chew.

It's grand to be a Minister
  And travel like a swell,
And tell the central district folk
  To go to—Inverell.

It's grand to be a Socialist
  And lead the bold array
That marches to prosperity
  At seven bob a day.

It's grand to be an unemployed
  And lie in the Domain,
And wake up every second day
  And go to sleep again.

It's grand to borrow English tin
  To pay for wharves and Rocks,
And then to find it isn't in
  The little money-box.

It's grand to be a democrat
  And toady to the mob,
For fear that if you told the truth
  They'd hunt you from your job.

It's grand to be a lot of things
  In this fair southern land,
But if the Lord would send us rain,
  That would indeed, be grand!

Riders in the Stand

There's some that ride the Robbo style, and bump at every stride;
While others sit a long way back, to get a longer ride.
There's some that ride as sailors do, with legs, and arms, and teeth;
And some ride on the horse's neck, and some ride underneath.

But all the finest horsemen out—the men to Beat the Band—
You'll find amongst the crowd that ride their races in the Stand.
They'll say 'He had the race in hand, and lost it in the straight.'
They'll show how Godby came too soon, and Barden came too late.

They'll say Chevalley lost his nerve, and Regan lost his head;
They'll tell how one was 'livened up' and something else was 'dead'—
In fact, the race was never run on sea, or sky, or land,
But what you'd get it better done by riders in the Stand.

The rule holds good in everything in life's uncertain fight;
You'll find the winner can't go wrong, the loser can't go right.
You ride a slashing race, and lose—by one and all you're banned!
Ride like a bag of flour, and win—they'll cheer you in the Stand.

Gone Down

To the voters of Glen Innes 'twas O'Sullivan that went,
 To secure the country vote for Mister Hay.
So he told 'em what he'd borrowed, and he told 'em what he'd spent,
 Though extravagance had blown it all away.
Said he, 'Vote for Hay, my hearties, and wherever we may roam
 We will borrow, undismayed by Fortune's frown!'
When he got his little banjo, and he sang them 'Home, Sweet Home!'
 Why, it made a blessed horse fall down.

Then he summoned his supporters, and went spouting through the bush,
 To assure them that he'd build them roads galore,
If he could but borrow something from the 'Plutocratic Push',
 Though he knew they wouldn't lend him any more.
With his Coolangatta Croesus, who was posing for the day
 As a Friend of Labour, just brought up from town:
When the Democratic Keystone told the workers, 'Vote for Hay',
 Then another blessed horse fell down!

When the polling day was over, and the promising was done—
  The promises that never would be kept—
Then O'Sullivan came homeward at the sinking of the sun,
  To the Ministerial Bench he slowly crept.
When his colleagues said, 'Who won it? Is our banner waving high?
  Has the Ministry retained Glen Innes Town?'
Then the great man hesitated, and responded with a sigh—
  'There's another blessed seat gone down!'

Saltbush Bill on the Patriarchs

Come all you little rouseabouts and climb upon my knee;
To-day, you see, is Christmas Day, and so it's up to me
To give you some instruction like—a kind of Christmas tale—
So name your yarn, and off she goes. What, 'Jonah and the Whale?'

Well, whales is sheep I've never shore; I've never been to sea,
So all them great Leviathans is mysteries to me;
But there's a tale the Bible tells I fully understand,
About the time the Patriarchs were settling on the land.

Those Patriarchs of olden time, when all is said and done,
They lived the same as far-out men on many a Queensland run—
A lot of roving, droving men who drifted to and fro,
The same we did out Queensland way a score of years ago.

Now Isaac was a squatter man, and Jacob was his son,
And when the boy grew up, you see, he wearied of the run.
You know the way that boys grow up—there's some that stick at home;
But any boy that's worth his salt will roll his swag and roam.

So Jacob caught the roving fit and took the drovers' track
To where his uncle had a run, beyond the outer back;
You see they made for out-back runs for room to stretch and grow,
The same we did out Queensland way a score of years ago.

Now, Jacob knew the ways of stock—that's most uncommon clear—
For when he got to Laban's Run, they made him overseer;
He didn't ask a pound a week, but bargained for his pay
To take the roan and strawberry calves—the same we'd take to-day.

The duns and blacks and 'Goulburn roans' (that's brindles), coarse and hard,
He branded them with Laban's brand, in Old Man Laban's yard;
So when he'd done the station work for close on seven year,
Why all the choicest stock belonged to Laban's overseer.

It's often so with overseers—I've seen the same thing done
By many a Queensland overseer on many a Queensland run.
But when the mustering time came on old Laban acted straight,
And gave him country of his own outside the boundary gate.

He gave him stock, and offered him a daughter's hand in troth;
And Jacob first he married one, and then he married both;
You see, they weren't particular about a wife or so—
No more were we up Queensland way a score of years ago.

But when the stock were strong and fat with grass and lots of rain,
Then Jacob felt the call to take the homeward track again.
It's strange in every creed and clime, no matter where you roam,
There comes a day when every man would like to make for home.

So off he set with sheep and goats, a mighty moving band,
To battle down the dusty road along the Overland;
It's droving mixed-up mobs like that that makes men cut their throats—
I've travelled rams, which Lord forget, but never travelled goats.

But Jacob knew the ways of stock, for (so the story goes)
When battling through the Philistines—selectors, I suppose—
He thought he'd have to fight his way, an awkward sort of job;
So what did Old Man Jacob do? Of course, he split the mob.

He sent the strong stock on ahead to battle out the way;
He couldn't hurry lambing ewes—no more you could to-day—
And down the road from run to run, his hand 'gainst every hand,
He moved that mighty mob of stock across the Overland.

The thing is made so clear and plain, so solid in and out,
There isn't any room at all for any kind of doubt.
It's just a plain straightforward tale—a tale that lets you know
The way they lived in Palestine three thousand years ago.

It's strange to read it all to-day, the shifting of the stock;
You'd think you see the caravans that loaf behind the flock,
The little donkeys and the mules, the sheep that slowly spread,
And maybe Dan or Naphthali a-ridin' on ahead.

The long, dry, dusty summer days, the smouldering fires at night;
The stir and bustle of the camp at break of morning light;
The little kids that skipped about, the camels' dead-slow tramp—
I wish I'd done a week or two in Old Man Jacob's camp !

But if I keep the narrer path, some day, perhaps, I'll know
How Jacob bred them strawberry calves three thousand years ago.

Man from Goondawindi, Q.

I

This is the sunburnt bushman who
Came down from Goondiwindi, Q.

II

This is the Push from Waterloo
That spotted the sunburnt bushman who
Came down from Goondiwindi, Q.

III

These are the wealthy uncles—two,
Part of the Push from Waterloo
That spotted the sunburnt bushman who
Came down from Goondiwindi, Q.

IV

This is the game, by no means new,
Played by the wealthy uncles—two,
Part of the Push from Waterloo
That spotted the sunburnt bushman who
Came down from Goondiwindi, Q.

V

This is the trooper dressed in blue
Who busted the game by no means new
Played by the wealthy uncles—two,
Part of the Push from Waterloo
That spotted the sunburnt bushman who
Came down from Goondiwindi, Q.

VI

This is the magistrate who knew
Not only the trooper dressed in blue,
But also the game by no means new,
And likewise the wealthy uncles—two,
And ditto the Push from Waterloo
That spotted the sunburnt bushman who
Came down from Goondiwindi, Q.

VII

This is the tale that has oft gone through
On western plains where the skies are blue,
Till the native bear and the kangaroo
Have heard of the magistrate who knew
Not only the trooper dressed in blue,
But also the game by no means new,
And likewise the wealthy uncles—two,
And ditto the Push from Waterloo
That spotted the sunburnt bushman who
Came down from Goondiwindi, Q.

Lay of the Motor Car

We're away! and the wind whistles shrewd
In our whiskers and teeth;
And the granite-like grey of the road
Seems to slide underneath.
As an eagle might sweep through the sky,
So we sweep through the land;
And the pallid pedestrians fly
When they hear us at hand.

We outpace, we outlast, we outstrip!
Not the fast-fleeing hare,
Nor the racehorses under the whip,
Nor the birds of the air
Can compete with our swiftness sublime,
Our ease and our grace.
We annihilate chickens and time
And policemen and space.

Do you mind that fat grocer who crossed?
How he dropped down to pray
In the road when he saw he was lost;
How he melted away
Underneath, and there rang through the fog
His earsplitting squeal
As he went—Is that he or a dog,
That stuff on the wheel?

Saltbush Bill, J.P.

Beyond the land where Leichhardt went,
Beyond Sturt's western track,
The rolling tide of change has sent
Some strange J.P.s out back.

And Saltbush Bill, grown old and grey,
And worn with want of sleep,
Received the news in camp one day
Behind the travelling sheep,

That Edward Rex, confiding in
His known integrity,
By hand and seal on parchment skin
Had made him a J.P.

He read the news with eager face
But found no word of pay.
'I'd like to see my sister's place
And kids on Christmas Day.

'I'd like to see green grass again,
And watch clear water run,
Away from this unholy plain,
And flies, and dust, and sun.'

At last one little clause he found
That might some hope inspire,
'A magistrate may charge a pound
For inquest on a fire.'

A big blacks' camp was built close by
And Saltbush Bill, says he,
'I think that camp might well supply
A job for a J.P.'

That night, by strange coincidence,
A most disastrous fire
Destroyed the country residence
Of Jacky Jack, Esquire.

'Twas mostly leaves, and bark, and dirt;
The party most concerned
Appeared to think it wouldn't hurt
If forty such were burned.

Quite otherwise thought Saltbush Bill,
   Who watched the leaping flame.
'The home is small', said he, 'but still
   The principle's the same.

' 'Midst palaces though you should roam,
   Or follow pleasure's tracks,
You'll find', he said, 'no place like home,
   At least like Jacky Jack's.

'Tell every man in camp "Come quick",
   Tell every black Maria,
I give tobacco half a stick—
   Hold inquest long-a fire.'

Each juryman received a name
   Well suited to a Court.
'Long Jack' and 'Stumpy Bill' became
   'John Long' and 'William Short'.

While such as 'Tarpot', 'Bullock Dray',
   And 'Tommy Wait-a-While',
Became, for ever and a day,
   'Scott', 'Dickens', and 'Carlyle'.

And twelve good sable men and true
   Were soon engaged upon
The conflagration that o'erthrew
   The home of John A. John.

Their verdict, 'Burnt by act of fate',
   They scarcely had returned
When, just behind the magistrate,
   Another humpy burned!

The jury sat again and drew
   Another stick of plug.
Said Saltbush Bill, 'It's up to you
   Put some one long-a jug.'

'I'll camp the sheep', he said, 'and sift
The evidence about.'
For quite a week he couldn't shift,
The way the fires broke out.

The jury thought the whole concern
As good as any play.
They used to 'take him oath' and earn
Three sticks of plug a day.

At last the tribe lay down to sleep
Homeless, beneath a tree;
And onward with his travelling sheep
Went Saltbush Bill, J.P.

The sheep delivered, safe and sound,
His horse to town he turned,
And drew some five-and-twenty pound
For fees that he had earned.

And where Monaro's ranges hide
Their little farms away,
His sister's children by his side,
He spent his Christmas Day.

The next J.P. that went outback
Was shocked, or pained, or both
At hearing every pagan black
Repeat the juror's oath.

No matter though he turned and fled
They followed faster still,
'You make it inkwich, boss,' they said
'All same like Saltbush Bill.'

They even said they'd let him see
The fires originate.
When he refused they said that he
Was 'No good magistrate.'

And out beyond Sturt's western track,
And Leichhardt's furthest tree,
They wait till fate shall send them back
Their Saltbush Bill J.P.

A Motor Courtship

Into her presence he gaily pranced,
A very fat spark, and a bit advanced.

With a Samson tread on the earth he trod,
He was stayed and gaitered, and fifty odd.

And she was a tulip just unfurled,
The sweetest thing in the motor world.

Her body was one of which poets dreamed;
Eighteen—twenty, or so she seemed.

Her air was haughty, her spirit proud,
But properly governed, as all allowed.

'Pity,' he said, 'my sad condition;
My heart's in a state of advanced ignition.

'Ask me to do some desperate deed,
And I'll do it at once at my topmost speed.'

'Sir,' said the maiden, 'pray be seated;
I fear from your bearing you're somewhat heated.

'And I trust that a timely lubrication
Of throttle will cool your circulation.'

As a well-made mixture she indicated,
With joy and gladness he radiated.

'Oh, come,' said he, 'in this soft spring weather,
Let us run over the world together!'

But she slipped his clutch with a gesture mocking,
'Your heart,' she said; 'I can hear it knocking.

'You haven't the gear at my pace to last;
Both men and motors—I like them fast.

'And I think that in me you have missed your
mission;
You are only an old-style tube-ignition!'

With a sidelong motion he left the place;
For weal or woe he was off his base.

He drove his car to the cliffs of Dover,
Made one short circuit and ran her over.

And the stormy Petrol her rest is taking,
Where only the wild waves do the 'brakeing'.

Wisdom of Hafiz

My son, if you go to the races to battle with Ikey and Mo,
Remember, it's seldom the pigeon can pick out the eye of the crow;
Remember, they live by the business; remember my son, and go slow.

If ever an owner should tell you, 'Back mine'—don't you be such a flat.
He knows his own cunning, no doubt—does he know what the others are at?
Find out what he's frightened of most, and invest a few dollars on that.

Walk not in the track of the trainer, nor hang round the rails at his stall.
His wisdom belongs to his patron—shall he give it to one and to all?
When the stable is served he may tell you—and his words are like jewels let fall.

Run wide of the tipster who whispers that Borak is sure to be first,
He tells the next mug that he corners a tale with the placings reversed;
And, remember, of judges of racing, the jockey's the absolute worst.

When they lay three to one on the field, and the runners are twenty-and-two,
Take a pull on your self; take a pull—it's a mighty big field to get through.
Is the club handicapper a fool? If a fool is about, p'raps it's you !

Beware of the critic who tells you the handicap's absolute rot,
For this is chucked in, and that's hopeless, and somebody ought to be shot.
How is it he can't make a fortune himself when he knows such a lot?

From tipsters, and jockeys, and trials, and gallops, the glory has gone,
For this is the wisdom of Hafiz that sages have pondered upon,
'The very best tip in the world is to see the commission go on !'

Santa Claus in the Bush

It chanced out back at the Christmas time,
When the wheat was ripe and tall,
A stranger rode to the farmer's gate,
A sturdy man, and a small.

'Run down, run down, my little son Jack,
And bid the stranger stay;
And we'll hae a crack for the "Auld Lang Syne",
For tomorrow is Christmas Day.'

'Nay now, nay now,' said the dour gude wife,
'But ye should let him be;
He's maybe only a drover chap
From the land o' the Darling Pea.

'Wi' a drover's tales, and a drover's thirst
To swiggle the whole night through;
Or he's maybe a life assurance carle,
To talk ye black and blue.'

'Gude wife, he's never a drover chap,
For their swags are neat and thin;
And he's never a life assurance carle,
Wi' the brick dust burnt in his skin.

'Gude wife, gude wife, be not so dour,
For the wheat stands ripe and tall,
And we shore wi' a seven-pound fleece this year,
Ewes and weaners and all.

'There is grass to spare, and the stock are fat,
When they whiles are gaunt and thin,
And we owe a tithe to the travelling poor,
So we must ask him in.

'You can set him a chair to the table side,
And give him a bite to eat;
An omelette made of a new-laid egg,
Or a tasty piece of meat.'

'But the native cats have taken the fowls,
They have na' left a leg;
And he'll get no omelette here at all
Till the emu lays an egg!'

'Run down, run down, my little son Jack,
To where the emus bide,
Ye shall find the old hen on the nest,
While the old cock sits beside.

'But speak them fair, and speak them soft,
Lest they kick ye a fearsome jolt,
Ye can give them a feed of thae half-inch nails,
Or a rusty carriage bolt.'

So little son Jack ran blithely down,
With the rusty nails in hand,
Till he came where the emus fluffed and scratched,
By their nest in the open sand.

And there he has gathered the new-laid egg,
Would feed three men or four,
And the emus came for the half-inch nails,
Right up to the settler's door.

'A waste of food,' said the dour gude wife,
As she took the egg, wi' a frown.
'But he gets no meat, unless ye run
A paddymelon down.'

'Gae oot, gae oot, my little son Jack,
Wi' your twa-three doggies small;
Gin ye come not back wi' a paddymelon,
Then come not back at all.'

So little son Jack he raced and he ran,
And he was bare o' the feet,
And soon he captured the paddymelon,
Was gorged wi' the stolen wheat.

'Sit down, sit down, my bonny wee man,
To the best that the house can do—
An omelette made of the emu egg
And a paddymelon stew.'

' 'Tis well, 'tis well,' said the bonny wee man;
'I have eaten the wide world's meat,
But the food that is given wi' a right good will
Is the sweetest food to eat.

'But the night draws on to the Christmas Day
And I must rise and go,
For I have a mighty way to ride
To the land of the Esquimaux.

'And it's there I must load my sledges up
With the reindeers four-in-hand,
That go to the north, south, east, and west,
To every Christian land.'

'To the Esquimaux,' said the dour good wife,
'Ye suit my husband well!
For when he gets up on his journey horse
He's a bit of a liar himsel'.'

Then out wi' a laugh went the bonny wee man
To his old horse grazing nigh,
And away like a meteor flash they went
Far off to the northern sky.

When the children woke on the Christmas morn
They chattered might and main—
Wi' a sword and gun for little son Jack,
And a braw new doll for Jane,
And a packet o' nails for the twa emus;
But the dour gude wife got nane.

Old Schooldays

Awake, of Muse, the echoes of a day
Long past, the ghosts of mem'ries manifold—
Youth's memories that once were green and gold
But now, alas, are grim and ashen grey.

The drowsy schoolboy wakened up from sleep,
First stays his system with substantial food,
Then off for school with tasks half understood,
Alas, alas, that cribs should be so cheap!

The journey down to town—'twere long to tell
The storm and riot of the rabble rout;
The wild Walpurgis revel in and out
That made the ferry boat a floating hell.

What time the captive locusts fairly roared:
And bulldog ants, made stingless with a knife,
Climbed up the seats and scared the very life
From timid folk, who near jumped overboard.

The hours of lessons—hours with feet of clay
Each hour a day, each day more like a week:
While hapless urchins heard with blanched cheek
The words of doom 'Come in on Saturday'.

The master gowned and spectacled, precise,
Trying to rule by methods firm and kind
But always just a little bit behind
The latest villainy, the last device,

Born of some smoothfaced urchin's fertile brain
To irritate the hapless pedagogue,
And first involve him in a mental fog
Then 'have' him with the same old tale again.

The 'bogus' fight that brought the sergeant down
To that dark corner by the old brick wall,
Where mimic combat and theatric brawl
Made noise enough to terrify the town.

But on wet days the fray was genuine,
When small boys pushed each other in the mud
And fought in silence till thin streams of blood
Their dirty faces would incarnadine.

The football match or practice in the park
With rampant hoodlums joining in the game
Till on one famous holiday there came
A gang that seized the football for a lark.

Then raged the combat without rest or pause,
Till one, a hero, Hawkins unafraid
Regained the ball, and later on displayed
His nose knocked sideways in his country's cause.

Before the mind quaint visions rise and fall,
Old jokes, old sports, old students dead and gone:
And some that lead us still, while some toil on
As rank and file, but 'Grammar' children all.

And he, the pilot, who has laid the course
For all to steer by, honest, unafraid—
Truth is his beacon light, so he has made
The name of the old School a living force.

The Road to Hogan's Gap

Now look, y' see, it's this way like,
  Y' cross the broken bridge
And run the crick down till y' strike
  The second right-hand ridge.

The track is hard to see in parts,
  But still it's pretty clear;
There's been two Injin hawkers' carts
  Along that road this year.

Well, run that right-hand ridge along,
  It ain't, to say, too steep.
There's two fresh tracks might put y' wrong
  Where blokes went out with sheep.

But keep the crick upon your right,
  And follow pretty straight
Along the spur, until y' sight
  A wire and sapling gate.

Well, that's where Hogan's old grey mare
  Fell off and broke her back;
You'll see her carcase layin' there,
  Jist down below the track.

And then you drop two mile, or three,
  It's pretty steep and blind;
You want to go and fall a tree
  And tie it on behind.

And then you'll pass a broken cart
  Below a granite bluff;
And that is where you strike the part
  They reckon pretty rough.

But by the time you've got that far
  It's either cure or kill,
So turn your horses round the spur
  And face 'em up the hill.

For, look, if you should miss the slope
  And get below the track,
You haven't got the whitest hope
  Of ever gettin' back.

An' halfway up you'll see the hide
  Of Hogan's brindled bull;
Well, mind and keep the right-hand side,
  The left's too steep a pull

And both the banks is full of cracks;
An' just about at dark
You'll see the last year's bullock tracks
Where Hogan drew the bark.

The marks is old and pretty faint
And grown with scrub and such;
Of course the track to Hogan's ain't
A road that's travelled much.

But turn and run the tracks along
For half a mile or more,
And then, of course, you can't go wrong—
You're right at Hogan's door.

When first you come to Hogan's gate
He mightn't show, perhaps;
He's pretty sure to plant and wait
To see it ain't the traps.

I wouldn't call it good enough
To let your horses out;
There's some that's pretty extra rough
Is livin' round about.

It's likely if your horses did
Get feedin' near the track,
It's goin' to cost at least a quid
Or more to get them back.

So, if you find they're off the place,
It's up to you to go
And flash a quid in Hogan's face—
He'll know the blokes that know.

But, listen, if you're feelin' dry,
Just see there's no one near,
And go and wink the other eye
And ask for ginger beer.

The blokes come in from near and far
To sample Hogan's pop;
They reckon once they breast the bar
They stay there till they drop.

On Sundays you can see them spread
Like flies around the tap.
It's like that song 'The Livin' Dead'
Up there at Hogan's Gap.

They like to make it pretty strong
Whenever there's a charnce;
So when a stranger comes along
They always holds a darnce.

There's recitations, songs, and fights,
They do the thing a treat.
There's one long bloke up there recites
As well as e'er you'd meet.

They're lively blokes all right up there,
It's never dull a day.
I'd go meself if I could spare
The time to get away.

* * *

The stranger turned his horses, quick,
He didn't cross the bridge.
He didn't go along the crick
To strike the second ridge.

He didn't make the trip, because
He wasn't feeling fit.
His business up at Hogan's was
To serve him with a writ.

He reckoned if he faced the pull
And climbed the rocky stair,
The next to come might find his hide
A landmark on the mountain side,
Along with Hogan's brindled bull
And Hogan's old grey mare!

Sunrise on the Coast

Grey dawn on the sandhills—the night wind has drifted
All night from the rollers a scent of the sea;
With the dawn the grey fog his battalions has lifted,
At the scent of the morning they scatter and flee.

Like mariners calling the roll of their number
The sea fowl put out to the infinite deep.
And far overhead—sinking softly to slumber—
Worn out by their watching, the stars fall asleep.

To eastward where resteth the dome of the skies on
The sea line stirs softly the curtains of night;
And far from behind the enshrouded horizon
Comes the voice of a God saying, 'Let there be light.'

And lo, there is light! Evanescent and tender,
It glows ruby-red where 'twas now ashen grey;
And purple and scarlet and gold in its splendour—
Behold, 'tis that marvel, the birth of a day!

Song of the Wheat

We have sung the song of the droving days,
Of the march of the travelling sheep;
By silent stages and lonely ways
Thin, white battlions creep.
But the man who now by the land would thrive
Must his spurs to a ploughshare beat.
Is there ever a man in the world alive
To sing the song of the Wheat!

It's west by south of the Great Divide
The grim grey plains run out,
Where the old flock masters lived and died
In a ceaseless fight with drought.
Weary with waiting and hope deferred
They were ready to own defeat,
Till at last they heard the master-word
And the master-word was Wheat.

Yarran and Myall and Box and Pine—
'Twas axe and fire for all;
They scarce could tarry to blaze the line
Or wait for the trees to fall,
Ere the team was yoked and the gates flung wide,
And the dust of the horses' feet
Rose up like a pillar of smoke to guide
The wonderful march of Wheat.

Furrow by furrow, and fold by fold,
The soil is turned on the plain;
Better than silver and better than gold
Is the surface-mine of the grain.
Better than cattle and better than sheep
In the fight with the drought and heat.
For a streak of stubbornness wide and deep
Lies hid in a grain of Wheat.

When the stock is swept by the hand of fate,
Deep down in his bed of clay
The brave brown Wheat will lie and wait
For the resurrection day:
Lie hid while the whole world thinks him dead;
But the spring rain, soft and sweet,
Will over the steaming paddocks spread
The first green flush of the Wheat.

Green and amber and gold it grows
When the sun sinks late in the West
And the breeze sweeps over the rippling rows
Where the quail and the skylark nest.
Mountain or river or shining star,
There's never a sight can beat—
Away to the skyline stretching far—
A sea of the ripening Wheat.

When the burning harvest sun sinks low,
And the shadows stretch on the plain,
The roaring strippers come and go
Like ships on a sea of grain;
Till the lurching, groaning waggons bear
Their tale of the load complete.
Of the world's great work he has done his share
Who has gathered a crop of wheat.

Princes and Potentates and Czars,
They travel in regal state,
But old King Wheat has a thousand cars
For his trip to the water-gate;
And his thousand steamships breast the tide
And plough thro' the wind and sleet
To the lands where the teeming millions bide
That say, 'Thank God for Wheat!'

The Mountain Squatter

Here in my mountain home,
On rugged hills and steep,
I sit and watch you come,
Oh Riverina Sheep!

You come from fertile plains
Where saltbush (sometimes) grows,
And flats that (when it rains)
Will blossom like the rose.

But when the summer sun
Gleams down like burnished brass
You have to leave your run
And hustle off for grass.

'Tis then that—forced to roam—
You come to where I keep,
Here in my mountain home,
A boarding-house for sheep.

Around me where I sit
The wary wombat goes,
A beast of little wit
But what he knows, he *knows.*

The very same remark
Applies to me also,
I don't give out a spark,
But what I know, I *know.*

My brain perhaps would show
No convolutions deep;
But anyhow I know
The way to handle sheep.

These Riverina cracks,
  They do not care to ride
The half-inch hanging tracks
  Along the mountain side.

Their horses shake with fear
  When loosened boulders go,
With leaps, like startled deer,
  Down to the gulfs below.

Their very dogs will shirk,
  And drop their tails in fright
When asked to go and work
  A mob that's out of sight.

My little collie pup
  Works silently and wide,
You'll see her climbing up
  Along the mountain side.

As silent as a fox
  You'll see her come and go
A shadow through the rocks
  Where ash and messmate grow.

Then, lost to sight and sound
  Behind some rugged steep,
She works her way around
  And gathers up the sheep.

And working wide and shy,
  She holds them rounded up.
The cash ain't coined to buy
  That little collie pup.

And so I draw a screw
  For self and dog and keep
To boundary ride for you,
  Oh Riverina Sheep!

And when the autumn rain
  Has made the herbage grow,
You travel off again,
  And glad—no doubt—to go!

But some are left behind
  Around the mountain's spread,
For those we cannot find
  We put them down as dead.

But when we say *adieu*
  And close the boarding job,
I always find a few
  Fresh earmarks in my mob.

So what with those I sell,
  And what with those I keep,
You pay me pretty well,
  Oh Riverina Sheep!

It's up to me to shout
  Before we say goodbye—
'Here's to a howlin' drought
  All west of Gundagai!'

Australia Today 1916

They came from the lower levels
Deep down in the Brilliant mine;
From the wastes where the whirlwind revels,
Whirling the leaves of pine.

On the western plains, where the Darling flows,
And the dust storms wheel and shift,
The teamster loosened his yokes and bows,
And turned his team adrift.

On the western stations, far and wide,
There's many an empty pen,
For the 'ringers' have cast the machines aside
And answered the call for men.

On the lucerne flats where the stream runs slow,
And the Hunter finds the sea,
The women are driving the mowers now,
With the children at their knee.

For the men have gone, as a man must go,
At the call of the rolling drums;
For the men have sworn that the Turks shall know
When the old battalion comes.

Column of companies by the right,
Steady in strong array,
With the sun on the bayonets gleaming bright,
The battalion marched away.

They battled, the old battalion,
Through the toil of the training camps,
Sweated and strove at lectures,
By the light of the stinking lamps.

Marching, shooting, and drilling;
Steady and slow and stern;
Awkward and strange, but willing
All of their job to learn.

Learning to use the rifle;
Learning to use the spade;
Deeming fatigue a trifle
During each long parade.

Till at last they welded
Into a concrete whole,
And there grew in the old battalion
A kind of battalion's soul.

Brotherhood never was like it;
Friendship is not the word;
But deep in that body of marching men
The soul of a nation stirred.

And like one man with a single thought
Cheery and confident;
Ready for all that the future brought,
The old battalion went.

Column of companies by the right,
Steady in strong array,
With the sun on the bayonets gleaming bright,
The battalion marched away.

How shall we tell of their landing
By the hills where the foe were spread,
And the track of the old battalion
Was marked by the Turkish dead?

With the dash that discipline teaches,
Though the hail of the shrapnel flew,
And the forts were raking the beaches,
And the toll of the dead men grew.

They fixed their grip on the gaunt hillside
With a pluck that has won them fame;
And the home-folks know that the dead men died
For the pride of Australia's name.

Column of companies by the right,
To the beat of the rolling drums;
With honours gained in a stirring fight
The Old Battalion comes!

A Ballad of Ducks

The railway rattled and roared and swung
With jolting carriage and bumping trucks.
The sun, like a billiard red ball, hung
In the western sky: and the tireless tongue
Of the wild-eyed man in the corner told
This terrible tale of the days of old,
And the party that ought to have kept the ducks.

'Well, it ain't all joy bein' on the land
With an overdraft that'd knock you flat;
And the rabbits have pretty well took command;
But the hardest thing for a man to stand
Is the feller who says, "Well, I told you so!
You should ha' done this way, don't you know!"
I could lay a bait for a man like that.

'The grasshoppers struck us in ninety-one
And what they leave—well, it ain't *de luxe.*
But a growlin' fault-findin' son of a gun
Who'd lent some money to stock our run—
I said they'd eaten what grass we had—
Says he, "Your management's very bad,
You had a right to have kept some ducks!"

'To have kept some ducks! And the place was white!
Wherever you went you had to tread
On grasshoppers guzzlin' day and night;
And when with a swoosh they rose in flight,
If you didn't look out for yourself they'd fly
Like bullets into your open eye
And knock it out of the back of your head.

'There isn't a turkey or goose or swan,
Or a duck that quacks, or a hen that clucks,
Can make a difference on a run
When a grasshopper plague has once begun;
"If you'd finance us," I says, "I'd buy
Ten thousand emus and have a try;
The job," I says, "is too big for ducks!

' "You must fetch a duck when you come to stay;
A great big duck—a Muscovy toff—
Ready and fit," I says, "for the fray;
And if the grasshoppers come our way
You turn your duck into the lucerne patch,
And I'd be ready to make a match
That the grasshoppers eats his feathers off!"

'He came to visit us by and by,
And it just so happened one day in spring
A kind of cloud came over the sky—
A wall of grasshoppers nine miles high,
And nine miles thick, and nine hundred wide,
Flyin' in regiments, side by side,
And eatin' up every living thing.

'All day long, like a shower of rain,
You'd hear 'em smackin' against the wall,
Tap, tap, tap, on the window pane,
And they'd rise and jump at the house again
Till their crippled carcases piled outside.
But what did it matter if thousands died—
A million wouldn't be missed at all.

'We were drinkin' grasshoppers—so to speak—
Till we skimmed their carcases off the spring;
And they fell so thick in the station creek
They choked the waterholes all the week.
There was scarcely room for a trout to rise,
And they'd only take artificial flies—
They got so sick of the real thing.

'An Arctic snowstorm was beat to rags
When the hoppers rose for their morning flight
With a flapping noise like a million flags:
And the kitchen chimney was stuffed with bags
For they'd fall right into the fire, and fry
Till the cook sat down and began to cry—
And never a duck or a fowl in sight!

'We strolled across to the railroad track—
Under a cover, beneath some trucks,
I sees a feather and hears a quack;
I stoops and I pulls the tarpaulin back—
Every duck in the place was there,
No good to them was the open air.
"Mister", I says, "There's your blanky ducks!" '

A Grain of Desert Sand

Beneath the blue Egyptian skies,
With ramp and roller, guide and stay,
I saw the Pyramids arise
And I shall see them pass away.

I watched when Alexander passed;
I saw Napoleon's flag unfurled—
The greatest and perhaps the last
Of men whose footsteps shook the world.

To each his hour of pride and place,
Arab and Persian, Greek and Jew;
Mahomet trod upon my face,
Darius spurned me with his shoe.

And yet I am not Priest or King,
Sultan or Chief in high command.
I am that one unchanging thing,
A grain of desert sand.

Swinging the Lead

Army slang for malingering.

Said the soldier to the Surgeon,
"I've got noises in me head
And a kind o' filled up feeling after every time I'm fed
I can sleep all night on picket, but I can't sleep in my bed".
And the Surgeon said,
'That's Lead!"

Said the soldier to the surgeon, "Do you think they'll send me back?
For I really ain't adapted to be carrying a pack
Though I've humped a case of whisky half a mile upon my back"
And the Surgeon said,
That's Lead!"

"And my legs have swelled up cruel, I can hardly walk at all,
But when the Taubes come over you should see me start to crawl;
When we're sprinting for the dugout, I can easy beat 'em all"
And the Surgeon said,
"That's Lead."

So they sent him to the trenches where he landed safe and sound,
And he drew his ammunition, just about two fifty round:
"Oh, Sergeant, what's this heavy stuff I've got to hump around?"
And the Sergeant said,
That's Lead!"

Moving On

In this war we're always moving,
Moving on;
When we make a friend another friend has gone;
Should a woman's kindly face
Make us welcome for a space
Then it's boot and saddle, boys, we're
Moving on.

In the hospitals they're moving
Moving on;
They're here today, tomorrow they are gone;
When the bravest and the best
Of the boys you know 'go west'
Then you're choking down your tears and
Moving on.

Hawker, the Standard-Bearer

Harry G. Hawker was a pioneer Australian airman in the years leading up to the First World War and became a leading test pilot in England after the outbreak of hostilities. In 1919 while attempting to fly across the Atlantic from Newfoundland he ditched into the sea only 100 miles from the Irish coast and was rescued by a Danish tramp steamer. In 1921 he was killed during a practice flight at Hendon aerodrome.

The grey gull sat on a floating whale,
On a floating whale sat he;
And he told his tale of the storm and the gale,
And the ships he'd seen under steam and sail,
As he flew by the Northern Sea.

'I have seen a sign that is strange and new,
That I never before did see—
A flying ship, that roared as it flew,
The storm and the tempest driving through;
Now what would that be?' said he.

'And its flag was a Jack with stars displayed,
A flag that is new to me,
For it does not ply in the Northern trade,
But it drove through the storm-wrack unafraid;
Now whose is that flag?' said he.

'I have seen that flag that is starred with white,'
Said a Southern gull, said he:
'I saw it fly in a bloody fight,
When the raider *Emden* turned in flight,
And crashed on the Cocos lee.'

'Now who are these whose flag is the first
Of all the flags that fly
To dare the storm and the fog accurst
Of the great North Sea, where the bergs are nursed,
And the Northern Lights ride high?'

'The Australian folk,' said a lone sea-mew,
'The Australian flag,' said he.
'It is strange that a folk that is far and few
Should fly its flag where never there flew
Another flag!' said he.

'I have followed its flag in the fields of France,
With the white stars flying free,
And no misfortune and no mischance
Could turn them back from the line of advance
Or the line they held,' said he.

'Wherever on earth there's a rule to break,
Wherever they oughtn't to be,
With a death to dare and a risk to take,
A track to find or a way to make,
You will find them there,' said he.

'They come from a land that is parched with thirst,
From vast dry plains,' said he;
'On risk and danger their breed is nursed;
And thus it happens their flag is first
To fly o'er the Northern Sea.'

Though Hawker perished, he overcame
The risks of the storm and the sea,
And his name shall be written in stars of flame
On the heroes' scroll in the Temple of Fame,
For the rest of the world to see.

Cassidy's Epitaph

Here lies a bloke who's just gone West,
A Number One Australian;
He took his gun and did his best
To mitigate the alien.
So long as he could get to work
He needed no sagacity;
A German, Austrian, or Turk,
Were all the same to Cassidy.

Whenever he could raise 'the stuff'
—A liquor deleterious—
The question when he'd have enough
Was apt to be mysterious.
'Twould worry prudent folks a lot
Through mental incapacity;
If he could keep it down or not,
Was all the same to Cassidy.

And when the boys would start a dance,
In honour of Terpsichore,
'Twas just an even-money chance
You'd find him rather shickery.
But once he struck his proper stride,
And heard the band's vivacity,
The jazz, the tango, or the slide
Was all the same to Cassidy.

And now he's gone to face the Light,
With all it may reveal to him,
A life without a drink or fight
Perhaps may not appeal to him;
But when St Peter calls the roll
Of men of proved tenacity,
You'll find the front-rank right-hand man
Will answer: 'Here ... Cassidy.'

The Old Tin Hat

In the good old days when the Army's ways were simple and unrefined,
With a stock to keep up their chins in front, and a pigtail down behind,
When the only light in the barracks at night was a candle of rancid fat,
When they put the extinguisher on the light, they called it the Old Tin Hat.

Now a very great man is the C. and C., for he is the whole of the show—
The reins, and the whip, and the driver's hand that makes the team to go—
But the road he goes is a lonely road, with ever the choice to make,
When he comes to a place where the roads divide which one is the road to take;
For there's one road right, and there's one road wrong (uphill, or over the flat),
And one road leads to the Temple of Fame, and one to the Old Tin Hat.

And a very great man is the man who holds an Army Corps command,
For he hurries his regiments here and there as the C. and C. has planned;
By day he travels about in state, and stirs them up to rights;
Full early he toils, and late he toils, and sits up half the nights.
But an evening comes when the candle throws twin shadows upon the mat,
And one of the shadows is like a wreath, and one like an Old Tin Hat.

And a very proud man is the Brigadier, at the sound of the stately tread
Of his big battalions marching on, as he rides with his Staff ahead.
There's never a band to play them out, and the bugle's note is still,
But he hears two tunes in the gentle breeze that blows from over the hill;
And one is a tune in a stirring key, and the other is faint and flat,
For one is the tune of 'My new C.B.' and the other 'My Old Tin Hat'.

And the Colonel heading his regiment is the life and soul of the show—
It's 'Column of Route', 'Form troops', 'Extend', and into the fight they go;
He does not duck when the air is full of the 'wail of the whimpering lead',
He does not scoot for the deep dug-out when the 'planes are overhead;
He fears not hog, nor devil, nor dog; he'd scrap with a mountain cat,
But he goes in fear of the Brigadier—and in fear of the Old Tin Hat.

The Quest Eternal

O west of all that a man holds dear, on the edge of the Kingdom Come,
Where carriage is far too high for beer, and the pubs keep only rum,
On the sunburnt ways of the Outer Back, on the plains of the darkening scrub,
I have followed the wandering teamster's track, and it always led to a pub.

There's always in man some gift to show, some power he can command,
And mine is the Gift that I always know when a pub is close at hand;
I can pick them out on the London streets, though most of their pubs are queer,
Such solid-looking and swell retreats, with never a sign of beer.

In the march of the boys through Palestine when the noontide fervour glowed,
Over the desert in thirsty line our sunburnt squadrons rode.
They looked at the desert lone and drear, stone ridges and stunted scrub,
And said, 'We should have had Ginger here, I bet he'd have found a pub!'

We started out in the noonday heat on a trip that was fast and far,
We took in one each side of the street to balance the blooming car,
But then we started a long dry run on a road we did not know,
In the blinding gleam of the noonday sun, with the dust as white as snow.

For twenty minutes without a drink we strove with our dreadful thirst,
But the chauffeur pointed and said, 'I think—— ,' I answered 'I saw it first!'
A pub with a good old-fashioned air, with bottles behind the blind,
And a golden tint in the barmaid's hair—I could see it all—in my mind—

Ere ever the motor ceased its roar, ere ever the chauffeur knew,
I made a dash for the open door and madly darted through.
I looked for the barmaid, golden-crowned as they were in the good old time,
And—shades of Hennessy!—what I found was a wowser selling 'lime!'
And the scoundrel said as he stopped to put on his lime-washed boots a rub,
'The Local Option voted it shut, it ain't no longer a pub!'

'Twas then I rose to my greatest heights in dignified retreat
(The greatest men in the world's great fights are those who are great in defeat).
I shall think with pride till the day I die of my confidence sublime,
For I looked the wowser straight in the eye, and asked for a pint of lime.

That Half-Crown Sweep

A Tale of the Territory

The run of Billabong-go-dry
Is just beyond Lime Burner's Gap;
Its waterhole and tank supply
Is excellent—upon the map.
But, lacking nature's liquid drench,
The station staff are wont to try
With 'Bob-in Sweeps' their thirst to quench,
Or nearly quench, at Bong-go-dry.

The parson made five-yearly rounds
That soil of arid souls to delve
He wrote, 'I'll come for seven pounds,
Or I could stop away for twelve.'
But lack of lucre brought about
The pusillanimous reply:
'Our luxuries are all cut out,
You'll have to come to Bong-go-dry.'

Now rabbit skins were very high—
There'd been a kind of rabbit rush—
And what with traps and sticks they'd shy,
The station blacks were very flush,
And each was taught his churchman's job,
'When that one parson's plate comes roun'
No good you put in sprat or bob,
Too quick you put in harp-a-crown.'

The parson's word was duly kept,
He came and did his bit of speak;
The boss remarked he hadn't slept
So sound and well for many a week.
But Gilgai Jack and Monkey Jaw
Regarded preaching as a crime
Against good taste; they said, 'What for
That one chap yabber all the time?'

Proceedings ceased: the boss's hat
Was raked from underneath his chair;
The coloured congregation sat
And waited with expectant air.
At last from one far distant seat
Where Gilgai's Mary'd been asleep,
There came a kind of plaintive bleat,
'Say, boss! Who won the harp-crown sweep?'

Typographical

A Ballad of Burdens

The Editor wrote his political screed
  In ink that was fainter and fainter;
He rose to the call of his country's need,
And in spiderish characters wrote with speed,
  A column on 'Cutting the Painter'.

The 'reader' sat in his high-backed chair,
  For literals he was a hunter;
But he stared aghast at the column long
Of the editorial hot and strong,
For the comp. inspired by some sense of wrong
  Had headed it 'Gutting the Punter'.

A Job for McGuiness

McGuinness and his wife are leaving Australia because he can get no work, though his wife is offered plenty of employment doing housework. The poem would be considered racist today, but in the years between the wars when this was written, such views were fairly commonplace.

Oh, it's dreadful to think in a country like this
  With its chances for work—and enjoyment
That a man like McGuinness was certain to miss
  Whenever he tried for employment.

He wrote to employers from Bondi to Bourke,
  From Woolloomooloo to Glen Innes,
But he found—though his wife could get plenty of work—
  There was never a job for McGuinness.

But perhaps—later on—when the Chow and the Jap
  Begin to drift down from the tropics
When a big yellow stain spreading over the map
  Provides some disquieting topics,

Oh, it's then when they're wanting a man that will stand
  In the trench where his own kith and kin is
With a frown on his face and a gun in his hand—
  Then there might be a job for McGuinness!

To George Lambert

AN ESSAY ON AUSTRALIAN ART AND LITERATURE
IN RECOGNITION OF LAMBERT'S REALLY EXCELLENT PORTRAIT OF MRS PATERSON

Come all ye men of paint and pen,
Who toil with hand and brain.
Forsake the town and take the brown
And dusty roads again,
The tracks that we old-timers know,
Who showed you all the way to go
With Clancy of the Overflow
Across the Black Soil Plain.

The Weather Prophet

' 'Ow can it rain,' the old man said, 'with things the way they are?
You've got to learn off ant and bee, and jackass and galah;
And no man never saw it rain, for fifty years at least,
Not when the blessed parakeets are flyin' to the east!'

The weeks went by, the squatter wrote to tell his bank the news.
'It's still as dry as dust,' he said, 'I'm feeding all the ewes;
The overdraft would sink a ship, but make your mind at rest,
It's all right now, the parakeets are flyin' to the west'.

The Silent Shearer

Weary and listless, sad and slow,
Without any conversation,
Was a man that worked on The Overflow,
The butt of the shed and station.

The shearers christened him Noisy Ned,
With an alias 'Silent Waters',
But never a needless word he said
In the hut, or the shearers' quarters.

Which caused annoyance to Big Barcoo,
The shed's unquestioned ringer,
Whose name was famous Australia through
As a dancer, fighter and singer.

He was fit for the ring, if he'd had his rights
As an agent of devastation;
And the number of men he had killed in fights
Was his principal conversation.

'I have known blokes go to their doom,' said he,
'Through actin' with haste and rashness:
But the style that this Noisy Ned assumes,
It's nothing but silent flashness.

'We may just be dirt, from his point of view,
Unworthy a word in season;
But I'll make him talk like a cockatoo
Or I'll get him to show the reason.'

Was it chance or fate, that King Condamine,
A king who had turned black tracker,
Had captured a baby porcupine,
Which he swapped for a 'fig tobacker'?

With the porcupine in the Silent's bed
The shearers were quite elated,
And the things to be done, and the words to be said,
Were anxiously awaited.

With a screech and a howl and an eldritch cry
That nearly deafened his hearers
He sprang from his bunk, and his fishy eye
Looked over the laughing shearers.

He looked them over and he looked them through
As a cook might look through a larder;
'Now, Big Barcoo, I must pick on you,
You're big, but you'll fall the harder.'

Now, the silent man was but slight and thin
And of middleweight conformation,
But he hung one punch on the Barcoo's chin
And it ended the altercation

'You've heard of the One-round Kid,' said he,
'That hunted 'em all to shelter?
The One-round Finisher—that was me,
When I fought as the Champion Welter.

'And this Barcoo bloke on his back reclines
For being a bit too clever,
For snakes and wombats and porcupines
Are nothing to me whatever.

'But the golden rule that I've had to learn
In the ring, and for years I've tried it,
Is only to talk when it comes your turn,
And never to talk outside it.'

The Uplift

When the drays are bogged and sinking, then it's no use sitting thinking,
You must put the teams together and must double-bank the pull.
When the crop is light and weedy, or the fleece is burred and seedy,
Then the next year's crop and fleeces may repay you to the full.

So it's lift her, Johnny, lift her,
Put your back in it and shift her,
While the jabber, jabber, jabber of the politicians flows.
If your nag's too poor to travel
Then get down and scratch the gravel
For you'll get there if you walk it—if you don't, you'll feed the crows.

Shall we waste our time debating with a grand young country waiting
For the plough and for the harrow and the lucerne and the maize?
For it's work alone will save us in the land that fortune gave us
There's no crop but what we'll grow it; there's no stock but what we'll raise.

When the team is bogged and sinking
Then it's no use sitting thinking.
There's a roadway up the mountain that the old black leader knows:
So it's lift her, Johnny, lift her,
Put your back in it and shift her,
Take a lesson from the bullock—he goes slowly, but he goes!

Song of Murray's Brigade

Small birds singing in the tree tops tell
Where runs the river of my home
And the wistful wishing of the folk who love us well
And follow us wherever we may roam.

And our hearts go back to the folk beside the river
To the land where the sheep and cattle roam
It's a long, long job, but we'll finish it together
For every mile we travel leads us home.

No songs greet us for the birds are mute
The aeroplane's the only thing to fly
Upward to the pilot send a special brand salute
For we may need him badly bye and bye.

Soldiers singing as their fancies come
New songs, old songs, they sang another day
Thus they sing and march to the beating of the drum
Till orders come to put the drums away.

And our hearts go back to the folk beside the river
To the land where the sheep and cattle roam
It's a long, long job, but we'll finish it together
For every mile we travel leads us home.

Index of Titles

Index of First Lines